Called Out With

Called Out With
STORIES OF SOLIDARITY

SYLVIA THORSON-SMITH

JOHANNA W. H. VAN WIJK-BOS

NORM POTT

WILLIAM P. THOMPSON

editors

Westminster John Knox Press
Louisville, Kentucky

Book design by Jennifer K. Cox
Cover design by Kevin Darst

First edition
Published by Westminster John Knox Press
Louisville, Kentucky

Royalties from this book will go to Presbyterian
groups working for justice for lesbian, gay,
bisexual, and transgendered persons.

This book is printed on acid-free paper that meets the
American National Standards Institute Z39.48 standard. ∞

PRINTED IN THE UNITED STATES OF AMERICA
97 98 99 00 01 02 03 04 05 06 — 10 9 8 7 6 5 4 3 2 1

ISBN 0-664-25719-4

Library of Congress catalog card number 97-12817

Contents

Preface

In 1995, Chi Rho Press published a remarkable collection of courageous stories, entitled *Called Out: The Voices and Gifts of Lesbian, Gay, Bisexual, and Transgendered Presbyterians.* Those personal testimonies give witness to the pain, anger, hope, and resilience of gay, lesbian, bisexual, and transgendered persons who struggle for justice, dignity, and respect in the face of harsh, exclusionary policies of the Presbyterian Church (U.S.A.). Their voices resound with a willingness to serve God and their church. Their stories also stand as compelling evidence that the church, in refusing to honor their gifts, inflicts needless suffering, not only on those whose lives are deemed "unworthy" but on the whole community of faith, which is denied the ministries of many of its good and faithful members. Those who have known God's call in their lives are thus prevented from joyfully fulfilling it in the life of the church.

These faithful lesbian, gay, bisexual, and transgendered persons are joined in their struggle for justice by many heterosexual persons who repudiate Presbyterian policies that treat some people as second-class members and deny ordination privileges on the basis of same-sex affiliation and sexual expression. It is time for heterosexual witnesses to "come out" and tell their stories, boldly renouncing church policies that accord them ordination privileges that set them apart from their brothers and sisters. This book is a chorus of heterosexual voices who declare themselves to be "called out with"—called out as allies in solidarity with all who work for a more just and loving church.

The stories included in this collection are by no means a complete witness to the total number of statements that could be compiled to reflect heterosexual support for change in the church. These voices are but a reflection of the breadth of that support. Each of these stories is personal and unique; each one has been written in its own style to convey an individual perspective and message. Each story testifies to the power of transformation in the life of the storyteller. As a whole, these stories reveal a corporate journey to the awareness that *harmful church policies affect real people.* Furthermore, these writers give testimony to their discovery that life-giving joy is found by entering into the justice struggle of lesbian, gay, bisexual, and transgendered persons.

We offer the stories of our lives as evidence of our commitment to this struggle, and we will not rest until the Presbyterian Church (U.S.A.) is a hospitable, egalitarian community for all people.

Sylvia Thorson-Smith
Johanna W. H. van Wijk-Bos
Norm Pott
William P. Thompson

Foreword

→ JANE ADAMS SPAHR

Called Out With presents itself as compendium and complement to the book *Called Out: Voices and Gifts of Lesbian, Gay, Bisexual, and Transgendered Presbyterians*. Here you will read stories of friends, family, and allies who work beside lesbian, gay, bisexual, and transgendered people to help create a church that will one day be fully inclusive.

We believe the words and lives of the people in this book because each person has demonstrated, in her or his own way, that we are in this justice work together. Each person owns his or her heterosexual privilege. They have come not only to understand but to challenge the oppressive systems that keep lesbian, gay, bisexual, and transgendered people from leadership. In particular, they challenge the Presbyterian Church (U.S.A.). Keeping lesbian, gay, bisexual, and transgendered people from leadership tears at the fabric of their lives and affects their faith. These heterosexuals know that when one suffers, we all suffer, and they believe that the damage done to us in the lesbian, gay, bisexual, and transgendered community diminishes the fullness of their lives as well.

These authors are not patronizing, but are allies using their privilege to shed more light on the injustice caused by forbidding the calls of lesbian, gay, bisexual, and transgendered people of faith who want only to serve. From their own life stories, these authors have come to see lesbian, gay, bisexual, and transgendered people as family, friend, or member of their own faith community. They also understand and have responded to the mystery and sacredness of sexual spirituality, of what today is often called an embodied faith.

Together, as people of faith, we grapple with questions about partnership, identity, ethics, theology, and scripture, and we strive to live our lives with integrity. Together, we see each person's sexual orientation as one of the many gifts godde gives to each of us. A sexual spirituality, or a spiritual sexuality, can and does enliven our lives in forming our intimate relationships with godde and each other. A spiritual sexuality can be a resource for living with a sense of wonder, passion, hope, and integrity.

For so many, abuse and misuse of power have led to fractured intimacies and have broken the sacredness of connectedness. Society's rigid restriction of sexual mystery and intimacy to a "heterosexual only" privilege leads to the labeling of others as "developmentally arrested," "sinful," or "depraved." Our lack of knowledge about sexuality and particularly about sexual orientation plays havoc with all of us. Instead of learning from the tremendous store of resources and educational materials that are available, we rely on misinformation that promotes violence and gives some the license to abuse and, yes, even to kill lesbian, gay, bisexual, and transgendered people.

This moving book acknowledges that the lives of lesbian, gay, bisexual, and transgendered people, like those of our heterosexual brothers and sisters, are vulnerable, stable, loving, and wounded. However, the Lavender community and indeed all but the most conservative heterosexuals have come to the realization that second-class citizenship is no longer acceptable in a society crying desperately for tolerance and equal access for all. Action to level the playing field is what our authors here require, so we can work together as partners, not as pawns, to transform a patriarchal, hierarchical structure. These writers see us as persons of worth and dignity, as friends to be respected.

I am honored to recommend this book, as we all work together to become brothers and sisters in the faith. These loving and courageous allies have learned well that mutuality and right-relationship with lesbian, gay, bisexual, and transgendered people bring many blessings. Thank you, our ally-author friends, for raising the idea once again of honoring diversity and owning what heterosexual privilege means. Thank you for showing and modeling what might happen if faith communities explode the myths surrounding sexual orientation and offer the possibility of learning a truly alive, embodied, spiritual sexuality together. You give us hope that someday we all may actually share in this dream.

→ Jane Adams Spahr, who earned both master of divinity and doctor of ministry degrees from San Francisco Theological Seminary in San Anselmo, California, has served as minister at Hazelwood Presbyterian Ministry in Pittsburgh, Pennsylvania; assistant pastor at First Presbyterian Church, San Rafael, California; executive director of the Oakland Council of Presbyterian Churches; minister of pastoral care of Metropolitan Community Church of San Francisco; and executive director of Spectrum, Center for Lesbian, Gay, Bisexual Concerns (formerly "Ministry of Light"), in San Anselmo, California. She is currently lesbian evangelist for "That All May Freely Serve," a mission project of the Downtown United Presbyterian Church in Rochester, New York, in partnership with Westminster Presbyterian Church in Tiburon, California. Janie is one of four editors of *Called Out: Voices and Gifts of Lesbian, Gay, Bisexual, and Transgendered Presbyterians*. She is the mother of Jim and Chet; she is a teacher, learner, preacher, and friend.

Introduction

✦   ROBERT McAFEE BROWN

A Closed Transom

He started out by asking if I would mind closing the transom above my office door. That wasn't a difficult request to honor from an entering student at Union Theological Seminary in the early 1950s. Entering students seldom fit the mold of conventional preseminary training in those days, and they might not wish to display their theological ineptitude too widely. The transom was closed.

We talked a bit about the courses he was taking—Donatism was a difficulty, as I recall, but we both knew it was not refuge from the Donatists that he sought. It gradually came out, haltingly and with difficulty at first. He was a homosexual person. He had discovered this during his university years, but in addition to all the old confusions and delusions there was a new one. He had come to seminary to prepare for ordination, and he was discovering already from many sources that if he seriously pursued the ordination track with any denominational body, he was in for a pack of trouble. This was something he had not had to think through before; it was powerfully unsettling, and initially there was very little that the young Auburn Assistant Professor of Systematic Theology and Philosophy of Religion could offer by way of help.

The transom was closed on a number of subsequent occasions, and we discovered various ways, both directly from the seminary and from outside sources, to find help. The student came one afternoon a few months later in considerable agitation. The psychiatrist had proposed a new way to deal directly with the student's "problem." In a number of situations comparable to this, the psychiatrist had employed the services of a young woman whose professional line of work was helping young men who were having difficulty confronting their masculinity or lack thereof. It was proposed that she "help" the student establish in his own mind that he was indeed heterosexual by having sex with her and, given sufficient practice, he would make that his permanent sexual orientation.

This proposal was deeply distressing to the student since it struck him as exploitative of both himself and the woman, quite apart from the question of whether he wanted to make a decision to be heterosexual or simply wanted help in adjusting to being a homosexual person. If the student was upset, let it be recorded that the young professor was also upset, and the result of our ensuing conversation was that the student arranged to continue his counseling under different auspices.

The thing that stayed longest with me in reflecting on this episode was that the thought of being a lifelong homosexual person was apparently so repugnant, even to a psychiatrist of the early 1950s, that *any* kind of changing of the moral boundaries of sexual activity was justified if it relieved the seminarian of his current low self-esteem. I also reflected that I would not have been privy to any of the discussion leading up to this proposal, had not a personal relationship already been established between that particular homosexual and this particular heterosexual.

That, after all, is the purpose of this particular book, namely to encourage and cultivate a new openness between heterosexual and homosexual persons that will not "work" unless the ingredient of personal trust has become central.

Well-Trodden Paths

Where do we go from here, in what are now the 1990s? There are a good many suggestions that don't help much any more. A lot of the intervening discussion has become threadbare, worn out by unappealing conversation that has lost the power to convince. Look briefly at a few responses:

1. The typically Presbyterian approach to any problem is to refer to *the witness of scripture.* I am not about to dismiss scripture as a vehicle for seeking the truth, but I do point out, from experiences over many years, that on these issues scripture has pretty well been run into the ground, and that we must not claim too much for continued ploughing over the same territory. It will not do any longer simply to rehash the power of scripture if we are already committed ahead of time to how much we will put up for grabs and how much we will insist upon keeping in our use of scripture. Exegesis has become eisegesis—not so much what we draw *from* scripture as what we impute *to* scripture. Only to the extent that we are honestly and daringly ready to *listen for new insights* can we use scripture as a creative resource for a position on sexuality. This is not a no to the use of scripture. It is a no to irresponsible use of scripture.

2. A second arena of investigation has been *tradition*, the appeal of which is that of endless material, most of which we have not yet read, save as we have skipped through the church fathers [sic], or the Reformers, or even the mystics, looking for proof-texting possibilities.

Here we encounter a problem in our quest for certainty. The tradition, much to our initial dismay, is not carved in stone. Different portions of the tradition have had different meanings at different times. Who would claim that the tradition is absolutely clear and unchanging on, say, war or racism, let alone sexuality or ordination? It is only within the lifetimes of many of us that we have discovered that the tradition does not forbid the ordination of women. If we can find what we need to sustain an argument in scripture, how much more can we do so with mountains of tradition at our disposal. And how much more precarious does the position become, the more heavily we lean upon it for our doctrinal explorations.

3. But let us not be unnecessarily iconoclastic. For when we talk about the authority of conscience, and genuinely mean by it the *authority of an informed conscience*, we are beginning to see beyond the immediate horizons that hide more than they reveal. It is a short step to realizing that scripture, tradition, and an informed conscience remain as helpful tools, provided the adjective "informed" remains central. We need a new sense of care concerning all avenues that lead us toward truth, and I propose that in our new situation a good test would be for each of us to entertain, with true seriousness, the possibility that the positions we have already arrived at must be rethought *in toto*, entailing true risk and an acceptance of vulnerability. In a phrase that always makes us a bit nervous, Oliver Cromwell remarked, "By the bowels of Christ, I beseech you to consider that you may be wrong."

4. Perhaps at this time in history we must *listen first of all to our contemporaries*, and especially to the gays and lesbians within our midst. Otherwise the dialogue will be wooden and unhelpful. Let us take seriously the theme of this book, and the personal experiences recounted herein, so that as heterosexuals begin to listen to, share with, and reflect on the experiences and the stories of lesbians and gays, our dogmatically impenetrable walls will begin to confront new ideas, and we will find stereotypes crumbling and encounter a new level of sharing of the deepest things of the Spirit.

There can be change. There *is* change. The Spirit has not forsaken us, though in all honesty we could wish for clearer messages of such change. I offer an event from the General Assembly at Albuquerque, which otherwise I found terribly disappointing. When it came to voting that our church support the rights of gays and lesbians to share in the simple gifts of civil life and social equality, 56 percent of the delegates supported the action. Surely that would not have been possible five years ago, or even five months ago. Let us not build too heavy an edifice of trust on this slender reed, but let us accept it as a sign that our church can occasionally begin to think in new ways. Let us at least be emboldened to whisper to one another that tradition is alive and well.

5. But what if we come to the conclusion that significant change is *not* going to come, at least not quickly enough to justify our staying within the church? At some point along the way, we have to weigh the merits of "staying in" or "getting out." In principle it is conceivable that the institutional church has strayed so far from what we believe to be the truth of the gospel that we can no longer give it our support. It has happened many times before, that men and women have had to decide, with P. T. Forsyth, that "a live heresy is better than a dead orthodoxy" and act on the conviction.

We must at least be sure that we are asking the right question from the right place. Indeed, it may be, as Luther and Calvin and others have taught us, that we have misunderstood the true "location" of the church in our time, which may not be for the moment within the traditional institution, but "out there" somewhere waiting to be rediscovered.

No one can make a decision to leave or stay solely on the advice of another, and we must honor the fact that different individuals may have different timetables. What is appropriate, or even mandatory, for one, may not be so for another. Past history suggests that the burden of proof is initially, at least, on those who decide to leave and that it is important to work within existing structures as long as that is possible. Nor do we wish by default to grant more power to the opposition by surrendering our voting power. But for all of us, the question of leaving or staying is finally the province of the informed conscience, and *the overall question must remain a real question.*

Ordination— And a Few Roadblocks

Let us examine some scenarios for gays and lesbians seeking ordination and trying to use the available structures.

Whatever advances my own thinking has made since that day in the office in the early '50s have come not so much from reading books or attending lectures, but from ongoing contacts with gays and lesbians in the interval. Most of my ministry has been in seminary classrooms, and the issue of ordination began to be raised with increasing intensity during that period. It can be taken as a reliable guess that in a seminary class of one hundred students, at least ten to twelve will be homosexuals. And the church has treated that 10 or 12 percent with singularly hurtful attitudes and practices.

The scenario I have experienced as a teacher is that fears about lesbians and gays do not appear quite as formidable within the seminary as elsewhere. To put it bluntly: I sense more trust and support among seminarians of whatever background than is liable to be found in a denominational church. My education on this matter evolved as I had classes with gay and lesbian students enrolled. I learned most when I offered a seminar on something like "The Church and the City" or "Spirituality and Justice." In the latter seminar there were nine of us, three of whom were gay.

What did this do to the atmosphere of the classroom? It did *not* produce an atmosphere of "gays take over" or "every discussion of social justice ends up as a discussion of lesbian ordination." What *did* happen, in a very creative way, was that in addition to the "regular" topics of discussion, the same issues were seen in a new way, through the eyes not only of straights but of gays and lesbians as well. The dominant atmosphere (and I have searched long and hard for the right word) was increased *sensitivity:* sensitivity to the pain through which all sorts of people in the inner city were going; sensitivity to the fact that standing for justice almost always gets you in trouble; sensitivity to the spillover of a reality like unemployment in the lives of children; sensitivity to proposals for shared Eucharists; sensitivity, too, to a thoughtless comment that had an unfortunate double entendre at the end; sensitivity to the fact that "spirituality" could be an in-group activity for either straights or gays and lesbians; sensitivity, too, to the fact that the close friendships would become fragile when friends were in competition for the same postseminary jobs; and, of course, deep fear on the part of almost everyone that those who had not come out of the closet might be exposed without one's intention of doing so.

The above comments are not offered to suggest that gays and lesbians are somehow 100 percent gentle and thoughtful and sensitive compared to the boorish straights who ride roughshod over others, but to suggest that because of what they have gone through, the chances of sensitivity and understanding on the part of gays and lesbians are remarkably high. It is one of the ironies of the situation that in banning homosexuals from the pulpit and pastoral world, the church is denying itself a vast number of ordinands whose pastoral instincts are often higher than those whose instincts have not yet been tested in the crucible of pain.

But one cannot remain forever in the supportive atmosphere of the seminary classroom. Students are soon seeking jobs, and it is often by pastoral search committees that the deepest wounds are inflicted. Here is a student with manifold gifts—warmth of personality, a good mind, outstanding organizational ability, creativity in the pulpit, empathy at the bedside. All is going well, and then somehow the issue of homosexuality arises, and if the candidate reveals that he or she is gay or lesbian, that is the end of the love feast. Period. The institutional response by the pastoral search committee is absolutely clear: gays and lesbians are not going to be ordained. "If you reveal your sexual identity," they are told, "there is no possibility of ordination. Can't you find a job within the church that does not require ordination? Otherwise you will be hurt."

The student, sensing the injustice of the situation, may want to press the issue. The most sympathetic response goes, "If you are irrevocably set on ordained ministry, then whatever you do, *do not reveal your sexual identity.* You must keep your sexuality a secret. You must, quite literally, 'play it straight.' Pretend to be what you are not. Deceive your denominational leaders. Your only hope is *to lie convincingly.* Then you can become an ordained servant of the one who said 'I am the truth.'"

(I have been told on more than one occasion that putting the case in such a way sounds judgmental and harsh. My response: "The position *is* judgmental and harsh. It will remain so until a majority of voting church members come to agree with the assessment and change it.")

It is a scandal for us to claim to be an open and inclusive community, with room for all—when we are not. We make a distinction between "membership" and "ordination," denying the priesthood of all believers in a most un-Reformed way. We pretend that to welcome to membership but to deny ordination should be considered a satisfactory resolution of the problem. Such talk gives grounds for charges of hypocrisy in what we mean by membership. The church's stance is to rest comfortably or uncomfortably with the present situation and expect a homosexual to believe that being offered a second-class citizenship is sufficient. It is not.

Albuquerque

At this point some might claim that the proposed Amendment to the Form of Government adopted by the 208th General Assembly at Albuquerque (1996) changed the situation and made it possible for homosexuals to be ordained in clear conscience.

I want to examine this claim from the following perspective: I am sure that in voting for the new material in the Form of Government, the delegates were acting in good faith. I am aware that most—or nearly most—saw the proposed legislation as helping to resolve the impasse in our church and that it was offered as healing rather than destructive legislation. And yet the great majority of the delegates were genuinely and painfully surprised that their proposal to deal with compassion and creativity was not so viewed by the objects of the legislation, namely gays and lesbians themselves.

What was operating was not vindictiveness so much as sheer misunderstanding. Nothing could illustrate more clearly the need for this book, *Called Out With,* which pleads for heterosexuals and homosexuals and bisexual and transgendered people to become better acquainted *on a personal level.* Unfortunately, the General Assembly action has made crossing the sexuality gap even more difficult than before.

The proposed amendment offers the following paragraph:

> Those who are called to office in the church are to lead a life in obedience to Scripture and in conformity to the historic confessional standards of the church. Among those standards is the requirement to live either in fidelity within the covenant of marriage of a man and a woman, or chastity in singleness. Persons *refusing to repent* of any self-acknowledged practice which the confessions call sin *shall not be ordained* and/or installed as deacons, elders, or ministers of the Word and Sacrament. (Form of Government, G-6.0106b [proposed], italics added)

The creators of this paragraph, it should be noted, describe their work as an example of the church "acting like Jesus." Let us reserve judgment.

Many matters in the overall proposal are worthy of comment; my comments will reflect on how I see this proposal being heard by lesbian and gay Presbyterians. There is rigorous exactitude about which homosexuals may be ordained and which shall be barred from ordination. Elsewhere in the report:

> Homosexual orientation is not a sin; neither is it a barrier to ordination. However, the refusal to repent of any self-acknowledged practice that Scripture, interpreted through the confessions, calls sin [which includes homosexuality] bars one from office.

Things could not be clearer. There is no equivocation. The "rules" are clear. No matter how deep and God-centered a given same-sex relationship may have been, it must be ended totally, and not only ended totally, but repudiated and described by the word "sin." For years, such persons have been waiting for the church to give some recognition that God's love is expressed in many ways, and that the love two people have found together could be honored and affirmed by all of God's people. Let us assume that their relationship has been monogamous, there have been no "affairs," and that both partners claim the other as the place where God is most genuinely present for them.

And now, if ordination calls, all that was good must be denied. All that was affirming and creative must be ended. All that was so clearly lasting must be terminated. All that was beautiful must be defined as tawdry. The ongoingness of the relationship must be ended and never again experienced.

There are no words, in my vocabulary at least, to describe how destructive and un-Christian this seems to me. There is a total inversion of values. If such demands were made on a "Christian marriage" we would be aghast at the conditions demanded in order to "regularize" what had been a creative union between two people.

At some point, things went badly askew in our church, and we must hope that the rejection of the proposed "solution" to gay and lesbian ordination will start us on a new course. Not until then, I fear, can we begin to appropriate the description of the church "acting like Jesus."

What is the hurt that we inflict most deeply on gays and lesbians who are rejected for ordination? It is not that we accuse them of such things as corrupting the young, though such charges have been present in some Presbyterian discussions. Our real sin against them, I believe, is that we *depersonalize them,* we reduce them to something less than full personhood. They are members of a "class"—homosexuals—rather than being accorded full humanity and a place among those who possess both uniqueness and great worth. We are to recognize in all other persons a uniqueness derived from the fact that they are created in God's image. But somehow gays and lesbians do not merit such affirmation. As members of a "class," we treat them in such a way that their deficiencies are more important to us than their virtues.

Two Conclusions

Two matters still need attention. The first I raise with some fear and trembling, lest I be misunderstood. But the importance of the issue transcends my trepidation.

1. For many of us, heterosexuals as well as lesbians and gays, the matters under discussion here have assumed such unquestioned priority in our lives that the raising of other issues is sometimes looked upon as a betrayal. This is appropriate, given the intensity of hurt that needs to be overcome, and those who have been targets of the church's homophobia are entitled to offer rebuttal and present their own convictions in a positive light.

But all of us who are participants in the discussion need to remember that sexuality is not the only ethical issue deserving attention. A case can be made that *issues of justice* must be our basic concern, and that gender issues are most convincingly explored as one of the justice issues, *but not the only one.* To some, such a claim appears to propose that less attention be accorded to issues of sexuality. That is *not* what I am suggesting. What I *am* suggesting is that being concerned about sexual issues is a clear example of injustice within the church and the world and can be most creatively discussed and acted upon in that context.

In a complex world, none of us are entitled to be "one-issue" persons, to the exclusion of concern for other issues. We find that as we work on gender issues, their relevance to other issues becomes more and more apparent, and our understanding is enriched. The more we explore our own central concern, the more our sensitivity to other issues is deepened. We are not finished with sexuality until such issues as hungry and starving children, racism, patriarchal culture, and the biblical interpretation of poverty have captured our attention as well. What is being proposed is an enrichment rather than a diminishment of ethical concerns. There is no honorable way to isolate one of them and exclude others from the discussion.

An example of this interweaving is found in the recent task force report on sexuality (submitted to the General Assembly five years ago and roundly rejected) that proposed that the criterion of "justice-love" could be a basis for measuring the appropriateness of various kinds of sexual relationship. I believe that one of the great ironies of our Presbyterian history is that this theme from the rejected report will turn out in retrospect to be one of the most significant contributions to ethical reflection that we have ever made.

2. Finally, over the past few years, as we have struggled with the issue of sexuality in relation to ordination, there have been many harsh words, many bitter statements, and much impugning of the motives of others. Let no one pretend it is not so.

Partly as a result of the intensity of the attack on gays and lesbians, there has been an increasing recognition that we need to reflect further on such matters as confession of sin, reconciliation, amendment of life, and new beginnings. This is a genuine advance, but I am left uneasy that in church discussion and church publications, the mandates for confession and forgiveness and reconciliation seem to have been addressed almost unilaterally to those whom the church clearly believes to be in the wrong. We have even perpetuated this one-sidedness in the new proposal before the presbyteries: how do lesbians and gays make their way back into the church's good graces? Very simply: by confession of their sin, asking forgiveness, and promising amendment of life.

Where is any acknowledgment in this process that *the church itself* has sinned, and sinned grievously, in its judgmental attitude toward those who, with genuine "calls" to ministry, have found the doors of our churches slammed in their faces? Let a healthy dose of *the culpability* of heterosexuals also be acknowledged in subsequent treatment of this issue. Let us begin to spend less time cataloguing the sins of others and focus on our own corruptions of the faith, even when we may not like what we find.

At the end of the day, this can be efficacious only when *all* of us submit our pleas and petitions to God, and seek the divine forgiveness, without which any words we utter, any deeds we do, will lack power. But as we rediscover that it is only the divine power that avails to forgive sin, perhaps we can begin to seek, and even begin to find, the forgiveness for which all of us stand in such need, and, emerging from our recent baleful treatment of our brothers and sisters, begin to find ways to rebuild our lives, and the life of the church, not separated, but together.

✦ Robert McAfee Brown is Professor Emeritus of Theology and Ethics of the Pacific School of Religion. He is a noted speaker and author in the church worldwide. Among his many publications are *Theology in a New Key: Responding to Liberation Themes* (Philadelphia: Westminster Press, 1978), *Saying Yes and Saying No: On Rendering to God and Caesar* (Philadelphia: Westminster Press, 1986), and *Reclaiming the Bible: Words for the Nineties* (Louisville, Ky.: Westminster John Knox Press, 1994). He is married to Sydney Elise Thomson, and they have four children.

Stumbling toward Clarity

✤ JOHANNA W. H. VAN WIJK-BOS

Family

In 1981 I attended a conference to celebrate the anniversary of the ordination of women in our Presbyterian denomination; this celebration was
held in Syracuse, New York. After years of going to conferences, I remember only a few details of the event distinctly: a sermon preached, a presentation given, dinner with friends. One moment, however, stands out for
me with great clarity. It was such a moment as comes into our lives now
and then, a moment that perhaps from the outside has nothing to mark it
from other experiences and yet it has the power to change us forever.

We are in Syracuse, New York, in a restaurant, my friend Elizabeth and
I with a group of women. There is a busy hum of conversation, the place
is crowded, we feel at home with our convivial group. In the midst of the
chatter, Elizabeth reaches into her wallet and hands around a picture of a
young woman, smiling, on the steps of a house. "Here," she says, "this is
my partner." We hand the picture around and into the small hush that has
settled on us, Elizabeth remarks: "You know, this is the first time I have
ever been able to show a picture of my family in public."

It was a simple matter, simply presented without self-pity or great
drama, and it smote me with a force from which I will never entirely recover. In biblical Hebrew the word for "convert" means literally "to turn."
I made a radical turn that day and redrew the lines of my basic convictions
so they took a different shape ever after. My friend Elizabeth had shown
me with terrifying clarity an essential part of what it means to live a life
that does not conform to the norm. Even if she had a family, she was expected to hide this from the world and the church. She, who obviously
was as fond of her partner as I was of mine, who would speak of her with
the same amount of pride, the same mixture of admiration and exaspera-
tion, as I use to describe my husband, was never supposed to bring any
of these observations into the conversation. When others would be ad-
miring pictures of family, spouses or children, her picture would be seen

as destructive of family structure rather than supportive of it. And above all, she did not ordinarily have this simple joy, this satisfaction we get from showing to others the smiling faces of those with whom we live in closest relationship. All of this and more I understood in that moment when my friend felt safe enough to share the most important part of her life with us.

Assumptions and Norms

Strangely, the encounter in Syracuse also made clear to me how much I had subconsciously identified homosexuality with maleness. There may be a number of factors that account for my unexamined assumption, such as my being acquainted personally for the most part with homosexual men rather than women. I had grown up in a culture in The Netherlands that was in many ways more open and tolerant of differences, also in terms of sexuality, than that of the United States, and had as far back as I can remember always known men who were gay, or about whom it was known that they were. On the other hand, tolerance and openness did not preclude the overpowering heterosexism that is a part of the ideology of patriarchy everywhere. My patriarchal ideologies were so dominant that even in groups that differed from the norm, males appeared to be the norm!

When my husband, David, and I moved to Rochester, New York, in the mid-'70s, the United Presbyterian Church U.S.A. was beginning to grapple with the question of ordination for those who affirmed themselves as homosexual. My early religious context had been defined by orthodox Protestantism in the Calvinist stream of the Reformation. This tradition provided me with a solid foundation in the tenets of Protestant Christianity and with a deep reverence for the Bible, a reverence that was not sympathetic to literalistic interpretation. When Virginia Davidson at that time asked me to think through with her the issues related to the ordination of homosexuals, I was convinced of two things: (a) concerns about homosexuals had to do with males, and (b) the creation texts in the Bible in Genesis clearly included the female as created in God's image (see Genesis 1:27).

When I discussed some of my hesitations with Ginny, I remember her patient and interested response. She, much farther along than I on the road to subverting the patriarchal structures and ideologies, met me with understanding and kindness. I was at that time clearly no firebrand on the barricades, fighting to break down the walls heterosexuals had erected to keep the "sin" of homosexuality outside. Some years later, I was surprised to find that from the beginning of my teaching at Louisville Seminary, I experienced the trust of a few gay, very closeted, students. In this respect, I credit my early upbringing in an environment that was far less homophobic than American culture. Because of this upbringing the irrational fear and hatred that constitute such a great part of religious attitudes toward homosexuality had never become a part of my posture. When students took me into their confidence it was perhaps because they sensed that, whatever my reaction might be, revulsion would not be a part of it. I was always honored by their trust and often saddened by what I foresaw would be a difficult road for them in the structures of our faith.

I was stumbling toward greater clarity when Elizabeth showed her photograph and provided me with the push I had needed to cross the threshold from sympathy to support and advocacy. From that moment on I understood far better than before how our assumptions and norms are formed, undergirded, and perpetuated by the patriarchy of which we are a part and that is a part of us. Within my developing feminist consciousness, it was important to see the issue of homosexuality also and first of all as an issue about women and their place in the structures. Students continued to take me into their confidence, and eventually a few of them were women; some remained closeted then and afterward, some were wrestling their way with great pain and confusion to a clearer understanding of their own identity and their place in the structures, some came out not only to me but to their entire context—family, friends, acquaintances, and church family. I am these days mostly happy for these women and men and rejoice with them that they have found at least a moment of sanity in an insane world when they can voice their self-understanding honestly in the presence of another human being. Through them and with their help I am on the road to recovery from my own heterosexism.

Patterns of Patriarchy

In the spring of 1991 I was preparing to attend the General Assembly of our denomination in Baltimore as a commissioner. I read dutifully and informed myself as much as possible about issues that would come to the attention of the Assembly. One report that had my special attention was that produced by the Special Committee on Human Sexuality, a report on which we were to vote in Baltimore. David and I were profoundly moved by the quality and insights of this document. We observed to each other how the church at times really outdoes itself and exclaimed at the prophetic voice that we found present in the words of this committee. We were also afraid that the church would not yet be ready to hear and accept what was being said here. And it turned out as we feared.

At the time I thought one of the reasons for the church's refusal to accept the committee's report was the clarity with which it identified a patriarchal web of relations as defining all understandings and practices of sexuality. In the contemporary context, patriarchy creates a web of unjust relations of which homophobia is a part. In patriarchal ideologies, males provide the norm, and males are in charge of deciding sexual mores and behavior. In a society, culture, and religion where heterosexuality constitutes the dominant manner of male/female relations, males have the power to regulate these relations. It was the direct challenge to patriarchy and the call to approach homosexuality as a justice issue that struck at the deep structures of our self-understanding as a Christian community. The Baltimore General Assembly proved that the Presbyterians, at least, are not yet ready to deal with the patriarchal cast of all relations in the church.

For me, Baltimore was the first opportunity to stand in solidarity with all those deprived of ordination because of their sexual and affectional orientation. The moment when I could join the silent procession that wound its way up the center aisle of the gathered Assembly was the instant when I felt closest to God's presence. Next to me, waiting to walk also, was an elder-commissioner who had served with me on one of the standing committees of the Assembly. When we finally had made our way with the procession to the front of the hall and stood in rows facing the Assembly, I heard her whisper to herself, almost like a chant: "It won't be long now, it won't be long." In the end, the report of the Special Committee on Human Sexuality was defeated, but I am convinced that the words in it are not dead and the service done by the people who created this document will prove to be invaluable for the church in the long term.

The process is, alas, taking longer than my elder-friend in Baltimore thought. At the 205th General Assembly of our denomination in Orlando, Florida, I was invited to address the Standing Committee on Human Sexuality of the General Assembly. I spoke strongly from a Reformed biblical basis: "As a biblical scholar, I believe we have no ground to stand on when we exclude lesbian sisters and gay brothers from the full exercise of their rights and privileges in our denomination. This is not faithful to the biblical text nor to our Reformed heritage. To interpret the Bible in a rigid and literal fashion, without drawing on our knowledge, reason, and experience as these are guided by the Holy Spirit, is not in accord with Calvinist principles." Instead of considering the particular sexual rules and mores of biblical times, I suggested that it would be more appropriate to apply the principle of hospitality to the stranger. In the Bible, especially the Hebrew Bible, this directive permeates the text wherever requirements for the common life of the community are provided or a breach of these requirements is narrated, or where prophets speak of the unjust relations that prevail. I charged the Presbyterian Church (U.S.A.) in Orlando with not only refusing a welcome to many but with practicing estrangement. The biblical requirement is to know the heart of the stranger (see Exodus 23:9), that is to say, to walk where the stranger walks, to stand where the stranger stands. Since God is present with strangers in their state of deprivation, we stand and walk in this way in God's presence. Our denomination has practiced estranging people; not only our lesbian, gay, bisexual, and transgendered sisters and brothers are being estranged but also heterosexuals who walk where they walk, who know the heart of the stranger.

Marching in the Light of God

In the fall of 1994, Jane Spahr and Virginia Davidson visited Louisville and the seminary campus. In depriving Jane of her rightful call, the Presbyterian denomination has made her ministry available to a far greater number of people than would otherwise have been blessed by her ministry. This was indeed true on our campus in more ways than I can recount. The preparations for Jane and Virginia's visit had included a protracted struggle to obtain permission for Janie to preach in the seminary chapel. This long-awaited service took place on a Monday morning, not ordinarily a "chapel day." Approximately a hundred people came; students participated in the liturgy that they had created, and Janie preached. A group called the Janie Spahr Singers sang South African freedom songs. As we launched into "We Are Marching in the Light of God," the congregation rose spontaneously and began to dance. We sang and danced until we were out of breath. It tends to make me nervous when Presbyterians claim to have experienced the presence of the Holy Spirit, especially when they do this after returning from a General Assembly. There was, however, no doubt in my mind this time that we sang by the power of the Spirit and moved by the power of the Spirit and that it was the joy of the Spirit that filled our hearts. In our chapel that Monday morning we danced in the light of God.

Most recently, the General Assembly has decided to send to the pres-byteries what it voted down by 307 to 260 votes in Orlando: the addition of a requirement to the Presbyterian *Book of Order* that those called to of-fice must exercise fidelity in marriage or be celibate. The most offensive language occurs in the last phrase, which calls persons to repent of self-ac-knowledged practices that are called sin in the historical confessions of the church and bars them from ordination unless they repent. It seems to me almost obscene for the group that is practicing exclusion of its own sis-ters and brothers to call those who suffer from this injustice to repentance. It appears self-evident that the group in need of repentance is the one that has perpetrated the injustice.

There is an instructive story in the Bible about repentance, in the third chapter of the book of Jonah. At that point in the narrative, Nineveh en-gages in a full-scale turning around from its evil ways and from the vio-lence that was in its midst (Jonah 3:8). I invite us to look at Nineveh as in a mirror and ask ourselves where the violence that was typical for Nin-eveh occurs in our midst. Only if we can locate the violence can we turn from it in repentance. In our community, talk of repentance is coming as a directive from those on the inside toward one group that it has pushed to the outside. I wonder whether as a church we have any idea what re-pentance entails. The Presbyterian Church (U.S.A.) still has to repent and turn from past and present violence against women in its midst, forty years after it saw fit to call women to ordained office. I do not doubt that in time, the church will see fit to ordain those who are in their sexual and affectional orientation different from the majority. But will it also repent of the violence done to our sisters and brothers over the centuries, in ide-ology and practice? And if we are not ready to turn and repent, will not then the violence continue? That, I believe, is the real question before us.

But then, there is hope! We are, after all, marching in the light of God. If Nineveh could repent and turn from its violence, surely we can do the same! It may be an outrageously strange event, when those who have been bent on the oppression of their neighbor move in a completely new direction. But it could happen. If it could happen then, it can certainly happen now, here, in our midst, by God's grace.

→ Johanna W. H. van Wijk-Bos is Professor of Old Testament at Louisville Pres-byterian Theological Seminary. Her most recent book is *Reimagining God:*

The Case for Scriptural Diversity (Louisville, Ky.: Westminster John Knox Press, 1995). She is an ordained minister in the Presbyterian Church (U.S.A.). Her husband, A. David Bos, is also a professional minister and is executive director of Interfaith Community Council, a Community Ministry, in New Albany, Indiana. They have one son, Martin, who is twenty-two.

➤2➤

How My Mind
Was Changed

✦ WILLIAM P. THOMPSON

> *Do not conform yourselves to the standards of this world, but let God
> transform you inwardly by* a complete change of your mind. *Then
> you will be able to know the will of God—what is good and is pleas-
> ing to him and is perfect.*
>
> —*Romans 12:2, Today's English Version*
> *(emphasis added)*

During 1977 and 1978, I was serving as Stated Clerk of the General Assembly of the United Presbyterian Church in the U.S.A. By virtue of that
office, I was frequently invited to speak to various groups regarding issues before the church that were expected to be considered by the General
Assembly. When I was able to accept such invitations, I attempted to sum-
marize the background of the matter and the way it would come before
the Assembly. I sought to avoid taking sides in the ongoing debate.

The preeminent issue before the 1978 Assembly concerned whether or
not "avowed practicing homosexual" candidates could be ordained to
church office, as deacons, elders, or ministers of Word and Sacrament. Responding to invitations, I made several presentations on this subject without
taking either side. Then, as the Assembly neared, I was asked to speak to a
group whose positions, whether on public issues or on theological problems,
were invariably conservative. I agreed to speak and outlined how this issue
had been initiated, and now came before the Assembly. At the conclusion of
my remarks, I accepted questions. One of the first was, "How would you
vote on ordination?" I had not studied the merits of the issue, had not
formed an opinion on it, and certainly had not expressed a position on the
matter. In retrospect, I probably should have said just that. But I did not.
Even though I knew that many of those present considered me far too liberal, I felt that my spontaneous response would probably accord with theirs.
I responded, "I would oppose it." Thus I avoided immediate confrontation.

My contacts with homosexual persons to that date had been few. While
I bore them no animosity personally, I fear that my response was shaped

by "the standards of the world" at the time. I did not consider the fact that those standards were homophobic, nor had I attempted to understand the biblical passages relied upon by those who took opposite sides on the ordination issue.

The 1978 General Assembly adopted the same position that I had taken so hastily. It described its action as "definitive guidance." I was later asked to express an official opinion regarding the effect of that action. Giving such opinions was one of the duties assigned to the Stated Clerk. My response was that the "definitive guidance" was an authoritative interpretation by the Assembly of the *Book of Order* and therefore binding upon all governing bodies of the church. That opinion was later reiterated by several General Assemblies.

In the years that followed, I attempted to serve those who wished to change the "definitive guidance," as well as those who stalwartly supported it. As Stated Clerk, I was always committed to facilitating the efforts of individuals and groups to bring their concerns before the Assembly in a way that would make it possible for the Assembly to make an informed decision. During that period, the Assemblies did not waver.

After I retired from the office of Stated Clerk in 1984, I served for the next seven years in a voluntary capacity as the associate secretary of the World Conference on Religion and Peace, representing that nongovernmental organization at the headquarters of the United Nations in New York City. Since I had more leisure than I had previously enjoyed, I spent some time reflecting on the issue of the ordination of self-affirming homosexual candidates to offices of the Presbyterian church.

My informal study was stimulated by several reports in the secular media that summarized findings of researchers who had concluded that homosexual orientation was the result of identifiable physiological characteristics present from birth. While I recognized that these reports were preliminary and far from conclusive, I began to question whether Christians could categorize this sexual orientation as a matter of conscious choice and therefore volitional, which I understand to be essential to designate conduct as sinful. Since these early reports, subsequent studies have reported similar findings, but the scientific community does not yet consider the research conclusive.

During this period, I also turned to the biblical passages cited by advocates on each side of the ordination issue. As a person without academic training in the interpretation of scripture, I sought the views of recognized biblical scholars. Here I found respected scholars of the Reformed, as well as other traditions, taking diametrically opposed positions. I was left without clear evidence from those to whom we look for insights on the meaning of scripture. I recalled the most recent treatment of the manner in which we should approach this sort of interpretation as found in the Confession of 1967:

> The Bible is to be interpreted in the light of its witness to God's work of reconciliation in Christ. The Scriptures, given under the guidance of the Holy Spirit, are nevertheless the words of men, conditioned by the language, thought forms, and literary fashions of the places and times at which they were written. They reflect views of life, history, and the cosmos which were then current. The church, therefore, has an obligation to approach the Scriptures with literary and historical understanding. As God has spoken his word in diverse cultural situations, the church is confident that he will continue to speak through the Scriptures in a changing world and in every form of human culture. (*Book of Confessions,* 9.29)

Following this approach, I turned once again to the Bible, where I was challenged anew by Jesus' openness to persons whose conduct had prompted their contemporaries to call them sinners (John 4:7ff.; John 8:3ff.; Luke 19:1ff.; Luke 23:39ff.). Even among his disciples, Jesus recognized sinful behavior without banning those involved (Matthew 16:21ff.; Mark 10:35ff.). He invited all persons in need to come to him without limitation (Matthew 11:28). Later, the apostle Paul defined the Christian community as "one in Christ" without distinction of ethnicity, servitude, or gender (Galatians 3:28). I could no longer justify limitations imposed on the basis of sexual orientation.

By far the most persuasive experience of this period was my learning of the betrayal of Scott Anderson (by a person in whom he had confided). I met Scott when he was elected to the delegation of the United Presbyterian Church in the U.S.A. to the Governing Board of the National Council of Churches, on which I was already serving by virtue of office as Stated Clerk of the General Assembly. Scott was then a student at Princeton Theological Seminary. Despite his youth, Scott's leadership skills were soon recognized, not only within our delegation but also throughout the National Council of Churches. He received assignments normally given to more senior persons, and he fulfilled each of them with distinction.

After graduating from seminary, Scott accepted a call to serve as pastor of a Presbyterian church in Sacramento, California. When he had been there for a time, he invited me to visit the church and speak. I agreed to do so and included that stop on an extensive Western itinerary. While there,

I learned of the outstanding work that Scott was doing, and I sensed the high esteem in which he was held by his people.

Subsequently, I was saddened to learn that a counselor to whom Scott had gone in confidence had revealed to another professional the knowledge, gained in his relationship as a counselor, that Scott is gay. I was shocked when advised that the second person, who was engaged in a personal conflict with Scott, published this fact. Scott immediately resigned not only the Sacramento pastorate but also the ordained ministry of the Presbyterian church, and enrolled in a graduate business program. I also learned that many members of Scott's church attempted to dissuade him from this action, but to no avail. We are fortunate today that we may still benefit from Scott's skills as a lay person, but we have lost his unusually effective pastoral leadership as an ordained minister of Word and Sacrament.

Since that time, I have become keenly aware of the loss of countless other excellent candidates for ordained office in our church. They have exhibited the skills that would have recommended them, and many of them have responded to a deeply felt sense of God's call. Yet, because of the policy adopted in 1978 that "practicing" homosexual members of the church are ineligible for ordination, the church has lost this vast company of leaders. Indeed, that policy has been affirmed and elaborated upon as recently as the 1996 General Assembly.

In 1991 and for several years preceding, I served as clerk of the session of the Nassau Presbyterian Church in Princeton, New Jersey. I learned that several years earlier, the session had been impressed by the promise of a student at Princeton Seminary who had served as a seminary intern at the Nassau church. When he was ready to be presented to the Presbytery of New Brunswick for ordination, the candidate disclosed that he was gay. Nevertheless, the entire session attended the meeting of the presbytery to demonstrate their support, but the candidate withdrew and later was ordained in another denomination.

The concern exhibited by that session was felt throughout the Nassau congregation and was remembered by later sessions. From time to time, adult study opportunities were provided for members of the church to learn more about issues involved in the ordination of homosexual candidates. Among the speakers invited to address these issues was Scott Anderson. In the late 1980s, the session considered the possibility of proposing an overture to the General Assembly seeking to remove the prohibition against ordination of homosexual members. I served on the task force that finally produced a draft of such an overture in early 1991. This overture would have left the examination and determination of readiness for ordination with the governing body nearest to the candidate and, therefore, best able to evaluate the candidate as an individual. Candidates for deacon and elder would have to be examined by the session; candidates for minister of Word and Sacrament, by the presbytery. This proposal was later known as "local option."

When the draft overture was presented to the Nassau session, it was by no means certain that it would pass. Debate on the proposal was conducted in several successive meetings. When finally put to a vote, the overture was approved unanimously, with members of faculty and staff of both Princeton University and Princeton Seminary, as well as the clerk of the session, voting in the affirmative. This overture, later referred to as the New Brunswick overture, was considered (and rejected) by the General Assembly in 1993.

I have recounted how my mind was changed on this issue over a period of years, largely through factors outside of my control. I felt that God was nudging me in the new direction. I am now convinced that the Presbyterian Church (U.S.A.) will ultimately recognize that, like other members, its homosexual members are eligible to be ordained to church office, because I am persuaded that this is "the will of God—what is good and is pleasing to him and is perfect."

⤳ William P. Thompson is a lawyer who practiced that profession for twenty years. Active in the Presbyterian church, he was ordained a deacon and an elder. After serving on the General Assembly Council of the United Presbyterian Church in the U.S.A. for six years, he was elected Moderator of the General Assembly in 1965 and Stated Clerk of the General Assembly in 1966. He served in that office until 1984. Much concerned about the ecumenical participation of the church, he served on the Central Committee of the World Council of Churches (1966–1991), as president of the World Alliance of Reformed Churches (1970–1977), and as president of the National Council of the Churches of Christ in the U.S.A. (1975–1978). Now retired, he lives with his wife, Mary, in LaGrange Park, Illinois. The Thompsons have three children, all married, and five grandchildren.

⇒3⇐

Another Way:
Speaking the Truth of Our Lives

↝ VIRGINIA WEST DAVIDSON

> Life is too short to wear tight shoes.
> —*Grandma Ros*

When speaking to church groups in recent years, I frequently accompany the Rev. Janie Spahr, our evangelist, who is supported by the Downtown United Presbyterian Church in Rochester, New York, and the Westminster Presbyterian Church in Tiburon, California, and who goes forth to spread the good news of Jesus Christ. This program was begun in 1993 and is named "That All May Freely Serve." During our events, I often sense a question that no one quite dares to ask: "How did you, a snowy-haired 'het' (heterosexual), become involved in our denomination's struggle over homosexuality and ordination?" At this time in my life (I'm now eighty), as a woman of faith looking back and reflecting on my journey, the simple answer is: "It's God's doing, not mine!" My faith/our faith, and the faith of our foremothers and forefathers whose stories in scripture are our stories, too, inform my understanding of this journey. Stories of Abraham and Sarah, or Miriam and Moses, of Elizabeth and Zechariah, or Mary and Joseph—these are the faith stories that inform and shape my understanding of what it means "to be called."

There's another answer to this "how come" question. What follows are flashbacks, picking up earlier threads in my story, which begin to speak the truth of my life.

An early flashback: Only in hindsight have I come to realize that growing up in the first half of this century for "good girls" meant living a traditional script or story, though I never saw a written version. For middle-class families with daughters (I had two sisters), the script read something like this: Get an education, go to college, go to work until you "get a man," get married and settle down as a good wife and mother of the children you "get" after you are married. It's the "conventional marriage" story, or living the "erotic plot."[1] Women's behavior was strictly prescribed by our culture and our religious beliefs, often based solely on scripture.

In my case, as with other women of my age, World War II interrupted that script when I spent more than two years with the American Red Cross Clubs in Great Britain. They provided a home away from home for American troops on leave. With the ending of that long war, and the welcome era of peace on the horizon, to be married and settle down seemed to promise the best of times in that scripted story. And so Samuel Davidson (whom family and close friends always knew as "Davie") and I were married in 1945, beginning forty-one years of a richly blessed and memorable life together.

Another flashback: It's now October 1962. Davie and I are parents of four school-age children, three sons and a daughter, ranging in ages from eight to sixteen. I'm en route to my first day-long training session as the new program chair for the Women's Association of Brick Presbyterian Church. My car radio crackles this beautiful October morning with Cuban missile crisis news. There is talk of digging backyard bomb shelters. The news makes me shiver! I had been in bomb shelters in Britain many times during World War II. During that same time interval, the man who would later become my husband was "deploying" scientists to Oak Ridge, Tennessee, for secret war work: processing uranium for an atomic bomb, though I first learned this information after the war ended. Suddenly, on that bright October morning, I realized in a new way that my family and I, and yes, some wonderful Presbyterian women, were given only *this* day to live. I had better make it count! It was many years later, recalling this incredible moment in my life, that I understood another woman's wisdom. Carolyn Heilbrun has observed: "Men tend to move on a fairly predictable path to achievement; women transform themselves only after an awakening . . . *identifiable only in hindsight.*"[2]

Flashback 1967: A beloved family friend, a young assistant minister in our church, is seated with me in our living room one afternoon. Tears stream down his face as he tells me that he's a homosexual (people didn't speak of gay men then). Until that moment, I believed I had never known anyone who was gay. Years later, I realized that several men I had valued for their gifts as colleagues in my Red Cross work in Britain during the war years were gay men. *Only in hindsight!*

My friend, Bruce, told me he had been in counseling for five years, and nothing had changed. The dean at the seminary, whose help Bruce had sought while a student, told him not to worry. Bruce said that the dean, suddenly moving forward in his chair, and with unusual intensity and

animation, asked, while gesturing with his hands: "Don't you ever fanta-
size about women's breasts? Just date some girls and you'll get over those
feelings." Well, he hadn't. And he had concluded he could never change—
"This is who I am." Would I, or our family, suddenly shut Bruce out of our
lives? Of course not. Though I was stunned with his news at first, I was also
deeply touched that my friend trusted me. That he chose to risk telling me
his secret has since been one of God's mysteries in my life.

Through the intervening years, it has become clear to me that it's the
human encounters with those we know that make the difference. Someone who is gay, lesbian, bisexual, or transgender, or whose sibling or child
or parent is, one who is ready and has the courage to share the truth of her
or his life, changes our perspective and offers a new lens of understanding. Ours is an incarnational faith, for it is through our encounter with
Jesus of Nazareth that the Spirit leads us to say: "Yes, I believe!" My
friend's truth-telling foreshadowed what would become an irresistible
call for me in later years. *Only in hindsight!*

Another flashback: In the early '70s, the United Presbyterian Church in the
U.S.A. responded to growing pressures from women and people of color
for fair representation on its boards and agencies. As a result, I was one of
a number of women elected to the Support Agency of the General Assembly. I was also appointed to represent the Support Agency on the newly
formed Council on Women and the Church (COWAC). Thus began my involvement in the broader life of the denomination, which would give me
a critical understanding of how the church-as-institution functioned.

In 1974, I attended my first General Assembly as a commissioner, since
I was then moderator of our presbytery. Not unlike Elizabeth or Mary,
who were thoroughly startled by Gabriel's announcement of new life beginning in their bodies, so I too was startled when the newly elected Moderator, the Rev. Robert Lamar, appointed me Vice-Moderator of that Assembly. Strangely, or perhaps not, it was this Assembly at which David
Sindt first announced the creation of the Presbyterian Gay Caucus. Another openly gay Christian in our church! David stood in the atrium of the
Assembly Hall holding a sign that read: "Are there any other gay Presbyterians here?"

Two years later, I returned to the Assembly as a commissioner, endorsed by my presbytery as a candidate for Moderator—one of five. It
was 1976, the year the General Assembly was asked to give "definitive
guidance" to the Presbytery of New York City. That presbytery had a
fully qualified candidate, Bill Silver, who was under care, ready for
ordination, and openly gay. At a pre-Assembly press conference, we

moderatorial candidates were asked this first question: "As a member of your presbytery, would you vote to ordain a qualified gay candidate?" Three said they would not vote to ordain; the fourth said "yes" to that question, adding that the church knew precious little about homosexuality and needed to do a great deal of study. The fifth candidate didn't attend the press conference, and she was elected Moderator.

I was the candidate who said yes to the question about ordination. Because of my long friendship with Bruce, I knew I could not equivocate when answering it, nor did I wish to evade it. Six weeks later, during the United Presbyterian Women's gathering at Purdue University, Moderator Thelma Adair and the Church and Society Chair, Jeanne Marshall, asked me to chair the newly created General Assembly Task Force to Study Homosexuality. I accepted, with little hesitation.

Deep within me, I believe I knew that saying yes to that call meant embarking on an extraordinary journey as a woman of faith. Nine years after my friend Bruce had come out to me, I would become fully involved in this struggle for justice and the full inclusion of gays and lesbians in our church. Was all of this accidental? I now believe it was not. Were all of those flashback moments just random happenings or were they God's providential leading? I believe they were God's doing, as improbable and awesome as was God's news for Sarah when she and Abraham extended their hospitality to strangers "by the oaks of Mamre" (Genesis 18:9–15). I now am able to discern connecting patterns in what might appear to others as isolated events. It's God who calls us as people of faith, and we are free to say yes or no. It's God who calls us to partner with God's self to do the work of "hard love" together—not just simple caring—for the excluded, the hurt, the powerless around us. *Only in hindsight!*

Two years later, in 1978, the General Assembly reversed the majority recommendation of our task force—that homosexuality is not a barrier to ordination—and declared that noncelibate homosexuals may not be ordained. Following that action, I was sorely tempted to say: I've had enough! Yet God's call persisted. It was then that I chose my next steps: to begin my formal seminary education and to explore my own faith questions, which continued to burn within me after the work of the task force was completed. Yes, the call persisted. *Only in hindsight!*

My years in seminary, beginning at age sixty-two, were a blessed gift for me. In a more "normal" course of events, I might have been in seminary in the late '50s. Instead, I received a master of arts degree in church history and theology in 1988 just before attending my fiftieth class reunion at Wellesley College. I had finished my course work in 1983 but post-poned writing my thesis for three years because of my husband's failing health. Davie died in 1986.

Only in hindsight! Recently, I've reflected on how different my journey would have been had I chosen to attend seminary earlier in my life. In the 1950s, the scholarship and theology of white Euro-American males would have comprised the core curriculum. By the late '70s, however, feminist and other liberation theologies had begun to flourish. Women writers were producing impressive academic scholarship; lesbians and gay men were writing the truth of their earlier hidden lives. Among liberation movements in mainline denominations, Presbyterians for Lesbian and Gay Concerns was growing.

In 1978, following the General Assembly in San Diego, the session of the West Park Presbyterian Church in New York City, with the Rev. Robert Davidson as its pastor, declared itself to be the first More Light church in the denomination. A More Light church is one affirming openly and with self-awareness that "there is yet more light to break forth from the Word through the work of the Holy Spirit," a conviction attributed to the Rev. John Robinson, a Puritan pastor, in 1620. Faithful to that declaration of conscience, such churches will ordain "out" gay or lesbian, as well as bisexual or transgender, leaders to the office of elder or deacon. The session of my own Downtown United Presbyterian Church (formerly First, Brick, and Central Presbyterian Churches, now joined as one) made its More Light declaration early in 1979.

As feminist and womanist scholarship began to grow, the interconnections among issues of sex, race, class, age, heterosexism, and homophobia became more discernible and more troubling to those working to change the oppressing, patriarchal status quo. The decade of the '80s was also a time when the Presbyterian Church seemed wearied, possibly by its protracted failure to reach resolution on the increasingly troublesome issues of homosexuality and ordination. Yet the struggle for real justice and profound works of love continue. "*Definitive guidance* has become a thorn in our constitutional flesh which must be removed," commented a tall-steeple pastor to me in 1993. "Too many moderate church members of goodwill are embarrassed by the painful, destructive consequences of its enforcement. They're looking for a graceful way out." Such a way out, however, still eludes us, and efforts at retrenchment seem emboldened.

A final flashback, to November 1991: It was a miracle! The pastor nominating committee, which I cochaired, had come to a clear consensus on the

candidate to fill the third copastor position at the Downtown Church. After almost eighteen months of searching, the Rev. Jane Adams Spahr was
our unanimous choice. She had seventeen years' experience in ministry,
with qualifications strikingly matched to our needs. Would we eliminate
her only because of her sexual orientation?

Now five years later, the remainder of that story has become Presbyterian history. The congregational vote in November 1991 was a satisfy-
ing 90 percent majority on the second ballot, following an hour-long discussion during which members were able to speak the truth of their lives
to one another, with extraordinary passion. Pondering these events in my
heart, however, I now must say: it was not the Downtown Church and its
pastor nominating committee that called Janie Spahr. It was *God's* calling
to Janie which joined us in ministry. We didn't set out to do this thing;
God chose us, and though we struggled and were tested, we finally said
"Yes!" So it was when the Presbytery of Genesee Valley voted to concur
with our call to Janie; and again, later, voted not to rescind its earlier action. And so it was when the Synod of the Northeast Permanent Judicial
Commission concurred with the presbytery action.

Finally, however, in November 1992, the General Assembly Judicial
Commission voted to set aside the call. In concurring with the decision,
four commissioners wrote: "[W]hile the law is destructive of the peace,
unity, and purity of the Church, it is the law, [and] we are obligated to apply it." It seems that the church is still too much in collusion with our patriarchal culture, rather than daring to embrace the work of grace-filled,
compassionate truth-telling within communities of faith, in the presence
of the one Holy God, our true calling.

Mark's account of Jesus' resurrection tells us that when the Sabbath
had ended, Mary Magdalene, Mary the mother of James, and Salome
brought spices so they might go to anoint Jesus' body. On their way, they
asked one another: "Who will roll away the stone for us from the entrance
to the tomb?" (16:1–3). They *knew* it was a massive stone, yet they didn't
turn aside! Today, we thank God for growing numbers of More Light congregations, and firm supporters in other churches, who no longer ask that
question, Who will roll away the stone? For the question has now become
a proclamation for all whose hearts and passions have been awakened:
"Together, we will roll the stone away!" It's the Presbyterian Church that's
now sealed in the tomb. And those still judged to be a scandal by the denomination, joined by justice-seeking allies and supporters, will roll the
stone away!

We will roll the stone away! That is our calling. God grant us the courage to speak and act on the very truth of our lives!

✦ Virginia West Davidson is an elder and member of the Downtown United Presbyterian Church in Rochester, New York. Virginia and her husband, Samuel, now deceased, parented four children, a daughter and three sons. A graduate of Wellesley College, bachelor of arts in 1938, and of Colgate Rochester Divinity School, master of arts in 1988, Virginia cochaired the pastor nominating committee that called the Rev. Jane Adams Spahr to be copastor at the Downtown Church. In the former UPCUSA, Virginia served on the Support Agency, the Vocation Agency, and the Council on Women and the Church. She also served as Vice-Moderator of the 186th General Assembly (1974) and chaired the Task Force to Study Church and Homosexuality (1976–78).

Exodus from Homophobia

⤳ GEORGE R. EDWARDS

To be "called out with" suggests a foundational reality of churchly life. The New Testament word for church, *ekklesia*, means by derivation "called out." This "called-out-ness" is deeply personal. It is marked by dramatic moments of decision, moving toward a destination not disclosed at the beginning. Being called out, however, is not a summons into solitariness but into solidarity with others on this way. Many church people in our time, including myself, find the exodus from homophobia a significant rediscovery of ecclesial consciousness, not only in the personal domain but in the societal unity experienced with those whose outing makes them vulnerable to contempt because they refuse to accept their assigned confinement.

Growing Up in the Church

My father, John, was raised on a dirt farm near Jackson, Tennessee. At age sixteen he left, without regrets, the poverty and isolation of that place and went to Memphis. He found work opening boxes in the back of a hardware store. Behind a somber and rationalistic side, he harbored a good sense of humor. To my knowledge he had no church background. Although he never finished high school, he remained throughout life a devoted reader of Everyman's Library, a steadfast admirer of the rustic, agrarian Lincoln, and an avid supporter of Roosevelt's New Deal.

My mother, Analee, became a Southern Baptist through the influence of her father. Her first love from childhood was the piano. She played and later taught with a strength that mirrored her favorite composer, Beethoven, filling the house with music still audible in my head.

John would not surrender to the Southern Baptist style, but he finally agreed, to my mother's delight, to become a member of the Presbyterian Church U.S. He gave up Sunday golf. In due time we were full-fledged

Confederate Presbyterians: Sunday school, morning worship, evening worship, Wednesday evening prayer meeting, and youth fellowship (known as Christian Endeavor).

The Southern Presbyterian ethos was not quite equivalent to Southern Baptist revivalism, but they had a common denominator in the culture of the Bible Belt. After all, Billy Graham's wife, Ruth, was the daughter of a Southern Presbyterian missionary to China, Nelson Bell, M.D., a self-confessed fundamentalist about two generations before the current resurgence of the term. One does not control where or in what circumstances one is born and reared. When I, as a pious and impressionable teenager, heard the elderly Bell's expostulations on the virtues of fundamentalism, in the evening coolness of a Montreat summer, it attracted me.

Sex: The Sacred Taboo

Sex was a nonsubject in our family education. I grew up literally not knowing what a homosexual person was. Youth meetings and summer church camps offered now-and-then seminars and discussions on dating and marriage. But as a precociously religious boy, I failed to notice the naturalness or even the humorous aspect of sex. Under Catholic auspices, I could have easily become a candidate for the celibate life.

Sexual maturity and the attractiveness of girls imposed obvious dilemmas for my guilt-prone, Bible Belt outlook on the world of sex. Augustine would have been proud of me. Bothered in early dating by the scrotal pain caused by sexual arousal without ejaculation, I dutifully sought the advice of a physician friend of the family, who gave me this gentlemanly counsel: "Most boys just go ahead and relieve themselves." The remark went over my head. Untutored in the alternative of masturbation, I thought this was a suggestion to relieve myself through sexual intercourse, a solution wholly at odds with my conception of sexual probity.

Earliest Memory
of Same-Sex Conduct

My first awareness of same-sex conduct came during my freshman or sophomore year in college. A preministerial friend of mine told me about his experience after he was given part-time work in the English department to do typing and proofreading for a new faculty member preparing a book manuscript.

As they sat beside each other working on this project, the teacher put his hand on the student's inner thigh, moving it gently and affectionately toward his crotch. After this experience occurred again at a later time, my friend reported it to the college president. At the end of the semester the teacher's contract was not renewed. I raised no question about the outcome of the matter and regarded the president's action as appropriate and necessary. (A question I have today is whether events would have followed the same course if this had been an instance of *heterosexual* behavior.)

A Shocking Episode of Homophobic Violence

At the age of twenty-three, I was employed as an attendant at Eastern State Hospital in Williamsburg, Virginia. The place had a Bastille aura despite a spacious lawn well kept by patients able to mow and trim, with massive trees shading walkways for passing from building to building. Male and female sections were carefully separated by buildings on opposite sides of the extensive campus. There were occasional opportunities for social interchange between male and female patients: at chapel services conducted bimonthly by local pastors, an occasional dance, and a modest program of arts and crafts minimally staffed and equipped. But sexual activity was contrary to the institution's policy and consequently covert.

My work was mainly on one of two wards for the more disturbed male patients. One afternoon "Willie," recently discharged after a brief stay in the military, was brought onto the ward. Soon after, while I was on night duty, after the bedtime hour had passed, I entered the section to which Willie had been assigned and effected a coitus interruptus between Willie and another patient. My words were strict, but no physical coercion was necessary to accomplish my intervention. After the second episode and reprimand, Willie and his partner apparently observed the prohibition I had imposed.

One summer afternoon, I was summoned excitedly from the front of the ward because "somebody was gettin' mauled." I ran down the hall to the back porch enclosed with heavy mesh wire from floor to ceiling. A relatively new patient, John, muscular, stocky, about forty, had pushed an older man, Cecil, onto a wooden bench against the inner wall of the porch. Cecil's left leg below the knee was a wooden "peg"—symbol of a time and a poverty when modern prosthetics had not yet arrived. Like a pile driver, John's fists were smashing Cecil's face, now marred beyond recognition.

Cecil's head was whipped back and forth in helpless recoil with each smashing blow. Eyebrows and lips were deeply lacerated, bleeding profusely. I screamed John's name, angrily pushing him away from the older man, demanding a reason for his brutal conduct. "Because," he screamed back, "he's a goddamned queer!" John had unexpectedly come across Cecil in an act of fellatio with another male patient.

Needless to say, by this time my ignorance of homosexuality had been rudely shattered, and a sharp realization of homophobic violence had fixed itself on my memory. John's wrathful reprisal was a crossroad of conscientization for me.

A Night on the Big Town

A year or two later I was working at Goldwater Memorial Hospital on Welfare Island in New York. Bob and I worked on the same ward. He lived in town; I lived at the hospital. We became friends. His father was Jewish; his mother, Episcopalian. Still a Southern Presbyterian, I attended Madison Avenue Presbyterian Church on Sundays when free from ward work.

Bob wanted me to do the town one night. We walked the area around Fifty-ninth Street and about 11 P.M. sat down on a park bench. Two young women appeared and sat on a nearby bench. I talked about them a bit, but Bob wasn't looking that way. He laid his arm around my neck and draped his hand down on my chest. At that point I suggested that we walk over to the doughnut shop for a cup of coffee. After the coffee we parted for home.

A few weeks later at the hospital, he asked me if I would go with him to a room at the beach somewhere on Long Island. I hesitated, not wanting to disappoint or anger him. Then I said I thought that he was gay but I was not, and I stressed that we could remain friends but not lovers. So the beach trip did not happen.

Wrestling with Romans

My academic work as a professor of New Testament at Louisville Presbyterian Theological Seminary was very gratifying. There were many opportunities for ongoing study and engagement with a range of social concerns that are, in my opinion, rudimentary for thinking Christians in a time when extensive cultural dissonance makes urgent demands upon the church for moral decision. Our predicament can be expressed biblically.

The Protestant Reformation of the sixteenth century represented a shift from ecclesial power centered in papacy to a more autonomous and democratic authority centering in scripture. *Sola scriptura,* scripture alone, became the focal point of a cleavage in Christendom akin to the first-century break between Christianity and Judaism. Impulses of diversity proliferated and continue to do so as biblical interpretation recognizes that structures of religious tradition marking the various branches of Christianity are not only subject to criticism but experience collapse under the intense heat of multicultural social forces. The women's movement is a primary exhibit of disintegrative criticism and reconstructive charisma in which biblical patriarchy in church and family has fought a losing battle for survival. But defenders of biblical patriarchy are still at work, and the resolution of gender justice issues in the church is still pending.

It was in 1975 that I first sought to give biblical integration to my growing perception of homosexual persons as a group alienated, oppressed, and demonized by a tradition of churchly teaching resting on a few biblical passages consisting mainly of Genesis 19; Leviticus 18:22 and 20:13; Romans 1:26–27; 1 Corinthians 6:9–10; and 1 Timothy 1:10. Having taught Romans for several years and recognizing the centrality of that letter to the thought of Luther, I prepared a paper on the context of Romans 1:26f. and read it at a regional meeting of the Society of Biblical Literature at Vanderbilt University.

In 1975 my earlier assumption that the Bible was an objective storehouse of religious truths to be dug out by dependable rules of interpretation had undergone much erosion. Indeed, the historical-critical method of study had a very liberative impact on my earlier notions of biblical inerrancy. But it seemed clear in time that it was nearly impossible to expound the original meaning of each biblical passage in its own historical setting. Further, it could be shown that biblical writers themselves, citing previous biblical passages (as frequently happens in the use of Hebrew texts in the New Testament), often show little concern to set forth the intended meaning of the original author. For example, Paul does not use Habakkuk 2:4 (at Romans 1:17; Galatians 3:11; cf. Philippians 3:9) to set forth Habakkuk's ideas, but Paul's own, as one who believes in Jesus as the Christ, while taking up, as apostle to the Gentiles, the ecumenical vision germane to this apostolate. Thus, no interpretation of biblical texts, even translations of those texts, can escape the subjective ideas, interests, motivations, presuppositions, or aspirations belonging to the interpreter.

Recognizing the painful human consequences of traditional Christian use of Romans 1:26f. as an anathema upon homosexual persons, I argued that the damage of this traditional use of Romans was analogous to the use of the Bible to defend slavery, then segregation, as my Confederate forebears had done, or to defend male dominance in church and society as a biblically sanctioned and divinely ordained institution. I argued that Romans 1:26–27 is not, in context, a piece of moral exhortation but a rhetorically controlled composition. Paul "sets up" the boastful representative of legal righteousness only to cut him down in Romans 2:1ff., and Romans 1:18–32 should be viewed as rhetorical jousting with the legalists: the integrative and recurrent theme of Paul's entire mission and message.

Even without resort to the rhetorical underpinnings I find in the context of Romans 1:26–27, well-accredited New Testament scholars like Klaus Wengst (University of Bochum) and Robin Scroggs (Union Seminary, New York) have effectively countered traditional homophobic use of these two verses. Unlike many contemporary thinkers in psychiatry, psychology, and medicine, Paul assumes apparently that one abandons an innate heterosexuality and embraces the homosexual lifestyle. If the professional societies responsible for dealing with human sexuality advise us that sexual orientation is a constitutionally predisposed factor and not a matter of individual choice, are we then to anathematize the American Medical Association and write off psychiatry and psychology? Would not this be equivalent to the wisdom that the world must be flat because my backyard is flat?

There is no Hebrew or Greek word for homosexuality. The word came over into English (from German) only in the last decade of the nineteenth century. Some translators, with reason, refuse to utilize the noun or the adjective in rendering biblical texts. By forcing the word "homosexual" to conform to traditional homophobic connotations allegedly residual in millennia-old biblical texts, what kind of cultural dissonance can be expected except the cacophony, sloganeering, and disintegrative partisanship that now afflict our ecclesiastical discourse?

Further, Paul may well assume that idolatry is the root cause of the "Gentile" depravity deplored in Romans 1:18–32. When, however, homosexual people fully share in the worship and work of the churches and serve the most conspicuous and least conspicuous offices of the church with unusual skill and fidelity, are we to assign them to the fate of infidels?

An Oasis on the Way

The General Assembly of the United Presbyterian Church in the U.S.A. appointed a task force in 1976 to study "Christian approaches to homosexuality, with special reference to the ordination of avowed, practicing homosexuals." I was one of nineteen members of the task force, chaired by Virginia W. Davidson of Rochester, New York. Sharing in the sessions of that group was a great leap forward in my exodus from homophobia. The task force report was written by Byron E. Shafer, a professor of biblical studies at Fordham University. It is found in the 1978 *Minutes* of the General Assembly, pages 213–60.

The meetings of the group were in all respects well planned and executed, democratic, and candid. The final report affirmed that "The majority of the task force believes that homosexuality is not sinful per se and that therefore self-affirming, practicing homosexual persons may be considered for ordination" (1978 *Minutes,* p. 253). These are modest, carefully chosen words. They do not say that all homosexual practices, just as in the case of heterosexual practices, are morally right. The report also recommended that the ordination question remain within the jurisdiction of the presbytery as the *Book of Order* already prescribes. The General Assembly, however, rejected our report's recommendation.

The ordination issue was revisited at the July 1996 Assembly. While the affirmative report of 1978 received less than 10 percent of the Assembly vote that year, the affirmative rose to 43 percent in 1996. The present sociopolitical climate of the nation does not encourage optimism about the outcome of presbytery votes on the matter prior to the 1997 Assembly, but hope, more patient than optimism, waits its time.

More Light
at the Grass Roots

My wife and I are glad to be a part of the only More Light congregation in Louisville Presbytery. It was in 1983 that the Peace and Justice Ministry Unit of our church (Central Presbyterian) prepared a More Light resolution to present to the session consonant with the intent of the 1978 task force, using these words: "We will welcome as full participants in the Body of Christ (without their having to hide or deny their sexual orientation or preference or affectional relationships) lesbian and gay persons who seek with us the worship and work Christ wills for the church."

Two members of our Ministry Unit felt that the resolution should go before the Mission Committee the next week before going to the session. It passed the Mission Committee unanimously, after some clarification was made, and finally on December 13, 1983, the session also gave unanimous approval.

Central Church has a growing constituency with a substantial number of gay and lesbian members. The cultural diversity of the church is very rich. At least two gay/lesbian theological students have served the church in various capacities for a year or more and still find a warm place in the memory of the congregation. Thirteen years as a More Light community gives us a solid basis for enthusiastic approval of an expanded, contemporary version of Galatians 3:28–29: "There is no longer Jew or Greek, there is no longer slave or free, there is no longer male and female, there is no longer gay or straight, for all of you are one in Christ Jesus."

❖ George R. Edwards, Ph.D., is Professor Emeritus of New Testament at Louisville Presbyterian Theological Seminary and also a member of the Presbytery of Louisville. He retired in 1985 after twenty-seven years of teaching.

⇒5⇐

Coming Out With

↗ KATHY LANCASTER

"Fag colors. She's wearing fag colors!"

Fourteen. High school sophomore. In the social big time: invited to a Wilmington, Delaware, weekend to visit a girl I'd met at summer camp. *Really* big time, by some standards, if you're from a modest family on Staten Island. Never mind the possibility of having fun: a square dance one evening, roller skating the next, even church on Sunday. Never mind the carefully packed wardrobe, the train trip, the trappings of being a guest. I had been invited to a Wilmington weekend.

I was wearing fag colors.

Was it a yellow-and-white-checked shirt with a green corduroy skirt? Or a green-and-white-checked shirt with a purple skirt? You know, I don't remember. Whatever ghastly combination it was, my hostess, in *her* fourteen-year-old sophistication, explained the whispers to me. She assured me that only fags, only fairies, wore that particular color combination. That she told me in the girls' bathroom at the high school after the square dance had started helped me not at all.

My delusions of societal grandeur were dashed. Did I survive the weekend? Apparently. Did I wear that combination of clothes again? Of course not.

What's a fag? My hostess never told me. But I knew it was awful.

"Will you interview to staff the homosexuality task force?"

Forty. Happy holder of a brand-new master of divinity degree. (Second career, third career, who knows?) In Pennsylvania to assist at my cousin's wedding. Ordination seven months away as I awaited the confirmation of my calling to connect the societal institutions of the church and the criminal justice system, through a local organization in process of formation.

And there was Dean Lewis on the phone, tracking me down on a summer Saturday to ask if I'd consider interviewing for a part-time, short-term assignment as staff to a national committee in process of formation.

The General Assembly had called for it, and a chairperson had been identified. The existing staff of the Advisory Committee on Church and Society couldn't handle an additional assignment. Could I?

"Thanks, Dean, but my calling is to criminal justice, not to homosexuality. Sounds like this would taint what I believe I'm supposed to be about," I responded.

Matter-of-factly, Dean explained: "Don't worry about it. If you're working in the church on social justice issues, you're already tainted, whatever the specific aspect of it is."

"Oh. Okay."

So there I was in late August 1976 in a conference room on the tenth floor of the "God Box"—a reference by some, in and out of the United Presbyterian Church, for 475 Riverside Drive, New York City; thought of by me, in my years across the street at Union Theological Seminary, as a bastion of bureaucracy that I would never want or need to enter. (But that's a different coming-out story, I suspect.)

And there were Virginia West Davidson and Dean Lewis, interviewing me for a job that I hadn't sought and had virtually no known preparation for, and that I wasn't sure I wanted—even though working until my real call came through would not be all bad, I supposed. A couple of weeks later, by default or fluke, whatever the competition was, I was offered the job. My earlier brief articulation of homophobia to Dean on the phone hadn't disqualified me, apparently.

So my ride began: roller coaster? merry-go-round? bucking bronco? white-water raft trip? Whatever the imagery, it was a wild journey. Still is.

And so, more importantly, the life of the United Presbyterian Church's Task Force to Study Church and Homosexuality began as well. Not with that name, certainly: the General Assembly instruction was to recommend the place of homosexuals—"avowed, practicing homosexuals," actually—in the life of the church. But, whatever the goals for the group's first meeting, one of its first outcomes was to clean up the language: homosexual is not a noun, it's an adjective. The noun is *person*. The adjectives related to personhood—blond, blue-eyed, left-handed, whatever—can then be introduced. But, regardless of the General Assembly's terminology, we were going to deal with homosexual persons.

And the task force, while instructed to recommend, was not going to decide anything; it was going to deal with process. And process, in this context, was study. For the church. For the task force. For its staff person.

So the learning began—and, for me, continues daily. The task force listened, discussed, listened, debated, listened, questioned, listened to an amazing array of persons coming before it: John Boswell, Robert Gould, John Money, a variety of specialists in biology, history, physiology, psychotherapy, process theology, history, on and on and on.

In a different phase, the task force listened and listened and listened to an amazing array of women, men, and teenagers who spoke during the series of hearings around the country. One woman called my office and whispered her concerns and anxieties about her protected anonymity if she testified. One man spoke from behind a curtain so the task force could hear but not see him in his literal closet. One angry church leader sought (unsuccessfully) to testify twice. Many told of their experiences as parents of homosexual children. Many sons and daughters could not tell their own experiences.

Can you ride a kaleidoscope? The changing people, the changeless stories, the anger, the pain, the insights swirled around the nineteen members of the United Presbyterian Church's Task Force to Study Homosexuality. And led to the yet-unresolved resolution in 1978, 1979, 1993, 1996, and many other points in between and in the future.

A portion of the swirling-around in which I lived during the Task Force's two-year life was the new and rare experience of meeting, talking with, traveling with gay men and lesbian women. Coming to know a little more than I had before, working through the initial (inevitable?) focus on sexual activity to the fuller essence of each individual. As *person,* far beyond the unfortunate "avowed, practicing" label the church insisted on bestowing.

Essentially—radically—I began to know and appreciate and love a far wider variety of people than my limited, fag-colored upbringing had ever permitted. Not just on the task force, or in the Advisory Council on Church and Society, or with the many church people whose lives the task force intersected. But the totality of my experience in that circumstance liberated me to see through and beyond my stereotypes, homophobia, discomforts, to the wider riches of diversity, celebrating God's creation of all and love of all.

Of course, as fine as that sounds, in many ways I still didn't get it. The local criminal justice ministry had been established, the Presbytery of Hudson River prepared to ordain me. And George Kandle, who was presenting the charge to the ordinand, reviewed some details about my calling. George was moving away from prison chaplaincy just as I was moving in, and our connections were more through his therapy training program. He asked me to tell him again about the task force and my work with it.

"No, no, George, my calling for ordination is to criminal justice, to

connect the church and the criminal justice system. *Not* to anything related to homosexuality!" Well, I was certainly clear about *that*.

Then. And now? Now I am not at all clear. My ministry—even with
moments of joy, challenge, satisfaction, glimmers of change and hope—
has been called into question by the institutional stance of the Presbyterian Church (U.S.A.) toward lesbian women and gay men far more dra-
matically than any earlier certitude I may have understood about my own
calling to serve God as a follower of Jesus Christ, as a minister.

The Halloween massacre—the announcement in October 1992 of the
Permanent Judicial Commission's decision against the calls of Jane Adams
Spahr and Lisa Larges—still sears my soul and my conscience.

As some of us in the Presbyterian Center in Louisville assembled in the
cafeteria that afternoon for a spontaneous time of prayer and lamentation,
I struggled to articulate what the Permanent Judical Commission's decision meant to me. A few years earlier my then-pastor had talked about the
self-immolation compact that he and several other clergymen had made
during their depths of despair over the United States involvement in Vietnam. No one was ever despairing enough to invoke that compact. But on
that October day in the cafeteria-chapel I viscerally understood their commitment; and the suggestion came to me that, in a different dimension, I
would wrestle with what I felt to be an ecclesiastical equivalent of self-
immolation, the laying aside of my ordination.

Janie Spahr, Chris Glaser, *many* other women and men with clear call-
ings from God, demonstrating gifts of the Spirit, proven dedication to
ministry—embodiments of the ordination vow to "seek to follow the Lord
Jesus Christ, love your neighbors, and work for the reconciliation of the
world"—are having their exercise of ministry thwarted because of an institution's focus on and rejection of their God-given sexual orientation.
And I, too well aware of my sinfulness and congenital ability to fall short
of the glory of God, continue as a minister of the Word and Sacrament in
the church of which I have been a part for more than half a century, in the
church that I love in my own way, in the church that is one part of the
body of Christ.

I continue to wrestle with that inconsistency, which continues to make
no sense to me. Wise, patient friends have counseled with me, and I well
understand that "self-imposed martyrdom" doesn't count. My standing
down from ordination would not change anyone or any circumstance but
my own. And I cannot measure where it would fall in my striving to be a
faithful follower of Jesus Christ.

So, for me, the question remains an open one. Among my prayers for the Presbyterian Church (U.S.A.) and all that dwell therein is the hope that this church will open the door wide to all to whom God has given gifts for ministry, including the gift of homosexuality, that together we may all serve with energy, intelligence, imagination, and love.

↣ At this writing—September 1996—Rev. Kathy Lancaster is Associate for Criminal Justice and editor of *Church & Society* magazine in the Social Justice Program Area of the National Ministries Division, Presbyterian Church (U.S.A.).

6

Shall We Dance?

✧ DUKE ROBINSON

Years ago, when I first heard of the need for heterosexual Presbyterians to support homosexuals in the church, it struck me as an annoying distraction. I had long operated on the notion that the church lives to expose injustice in the world, wrestle with secular powers, and heal the wounds of humankind. I also had never developed a taste for intramural skirmishes. So I had to relearn the message that even as we serve God's brutal and broken world, we are a part of it and must attend to our own injustice, our own destructive powers, and our own complicity in evil. I again had to take seriously Peter's words: "Judgment begins at the household of God."

As the church makes its way to the third millennium of the Christian era, I now contend that at the top of our agenda—along with justice for women, children, people of color, and the poor—we must put justice for homosexual people. The church's treatment of this minority, I believe, will either kill us or be our salvation. So how did I come to such a place?

I grew up during the '30s and '40s in a genteel, conservative Presbyterian home, in suburban Philadelphia. While our family felt no particular sympathy for homosexual persons, we harbored no hatred, either. We simply did not know anyone who would dare acknowledge being one. So while I'm sure my parents—decent, Bible-believing Presbyterians—were not affirming of homosexual persons, there was never any reason to talk about them.

I think I was a preteen before I became aware that there were people who were *different from us.* The older kids I ran with told me about *homos.* They said that instead of doing sex in the way I was dreaming about, those people, of all things, did it with others of the same gender (I didn't believe it at first, and I certainly would have said, *Please don't ask me how!*). In some way I came to the understanding that *homos* were sick or disobedient to God, or both. I also learned that, fortunately, they kept to themselves and didn't bother us, except for those who were *really weird* and were said to flaunt their abhorrent way of life in the streets of Philadelphia. It was about that time, too, I think, that I began to hear such terms as *faggot, fairy, queer* and *dyke,* but I never knew anyone to whom I thought they might apply.

Then, when I was fourteen, I had one of those experiences you never forget. A really big African American man made a half-hearted attempt to corner me in the underground men's room of the 69th Street station between Philadelphia and its western suburbs. I say half-hearted because even as he exposed himself and said in a deep, stern voice, "C'mere boy!" he left a path to the outside stairs, which I took at Superman speed. Having escaped, I remember thinking that if he enjoyed scaring nice, suburban white kids, he got his kicks that day from the look on my face. I also remember wondering whether he was one of *those people.*

Essentially, my youth and early adulthood were times of ignorance if not innocence. I spent four years at nondenominational Wheaton College near Chicago. Billy Graham remains its most famous graduate. No one at Wheaton ever admitted to being homosexual, perhaps not even to him- or herself. (It was difficult enough admitting you were heterosexual.) And I don't remember one comment about homosexuality during my time there. Not even snide jokes. Some of the boys, at that time, seemed *a bit strange*—they were more interested in prayer and sacred music than sports—but whether they were homosexual or not, I don't know. At the 1995 General Assembly, by the way, I learned that there is now an active underground Gay and Lesbian Wheaton Alumni Association, some members of which are former classmates of mine.

On graduating from college, I studied for two years at Fuller Seminary and then, deciding to return to the Presbyterian fold, transferred in 1956 to our seminary in Louisville. The only reference to homosexuality I remember at either school was by a Fuller professor. He commented briefly in class on the first chapter of Romans, shook his head once or twice and said, "Enough about that." It was negative but no tirade, just simplistic biblical interpretation. He obviously didn't like homosexuality, but he wasn't directing his disparaging remarks toward anyone in the seminary or the church; he was talking about *perverts* out there in the world.

I don't remember saying or hearing one word about homosexual persons in the first two congregations I served. Was I deaf? Do I, perhaps, have a bad memory? Was I asleep, for crying out loud? I certainly knew by then (late '50s, early '60s) that homosexual persons were not welcome in our Presbyterian family. I also probably would have acknowledged they must be there in the church someplace, but nobody talked about them and where they were I didn't have the faintest idea. All right, yes, I was asleep.

The fact is that, before the '60s, people in my social contexts were asleep with regard to a lot that went on in the world. Of course, even as I unconsciously was enjoying protection from the world, I probably helped put other people to sleep. The saddest part is that I was oblivious for years to the fact that, in the name of the man who treated women, children, the powerless, lepers, sinners, and other social outcasts with respect, the denomination in which I served as a pastor systematically, deliberately discriminated against its most devout homosexual members.

It was the late '60s before I began to awaken. Gays and lesbians outside the church helped that happen. And I didn't always like it. I remember visiting the University of California Berkeley bookstore, when a particularly animated and attractive young woman caught my attention. She was talking and laughing loudly in the checkout line next to mine and I couldn't help but notice her. Then, seeing almost immediately that she was holding hands with another girl, I instinctively squirmed and started to turn away. But before I could do that, the two of them, right there in front of God and half the student body, turned, embraced and kissed each other passionately on the open mouth. When they finally broke for air, they were giggling, enjoying each other. I almost had apoplexy.

Their intimate behavior was too public, they enjoyed its shock value too much, and I felt they were asking for trouble, like people who marry across racial, religious, or national lines. They mostly bothered me, of course, because they affronted my traditional, male-female, match-up world. Today, I think of the incident as two human beings enjoying their attraction—maybe their love—an attraction which at that time I was unfamiliar with, shocked by, afraid of, and therefore didn't like. While they shook my view of the world, it would be years before anything would shake my ignorance and complacency about our church's treatment of homosexual persons. Over the next decade, I would be focused on the important matters of Vietnam, Central America, and the environment, and with the day-in, day-out demands of the pastorate and of family life.

Actually, my awakening about the church began when I observed the 1978 General Assembly in San Diego. I was the proverbial donkey and that Assembly was the two-by-four that finally got my attention. I remember being bothered beforehand by the negative minority report to the Task Force Report on Homosexuality, the *definitive guidance* that would ban presbyteries and congregations from *ordaining self-avowed, unrepentant, practicing homosexuals*. I also knew the church was fearful about anything sexual. But I was not ready for such a cold, *definitive* rejection of the task force's majority report by a majority of commissioners.

Of course, by 1978, even I was awake enough to know we had homosexual church leaders. I also was aware that the church accepted them as
long as they hid their sexual identity. Some of us felt bad about our
hypocrisy, but we thought of ourselves as realists—we recognized the
conservative nature of institutions in general and the church in particular.
Also, to this point, most of us knew nothing of how homosexual people in
the church felt about serving in the closet. Unconsciously, I probably assumed they saw it as their cross to bear, but didn't give it much thought.
And now, the old ecclesiastical version of "don't ask, don't tell" was about
to pass away. Interestingly, a gay seminarian's simple desire for integrity
and his sensitive request for clarity on his call and potential for ordination
triggered its demise.

On the Sunday morning before I left for the General Assembly, just
completing ten years as pastor of the Montclair Church in Oakland, California, I brought celebrants up to date on the issue. I talked about its history and what I felt was at stake. I then predicted that, sadly, the Assembly would probably adopt the ordination ban. Of course, as it turned out,
I was right. I also was disappointed and disturbed.

Charlie Brown wants to believe that Lucy will be a big girl and not take
the football away as he's about to kick it. With the same spirit I went to
San Diego hoping the church would not play tricks on gays and lesbians
and would be more mature than it proved to be. Over the years, I had
been proud of Assemblies for their stands on behalf of justice. This Assembly took a step backward. What made it worse was that it seemed to
have no shame. I felt like the kid who is embarrassed by his parents. Even
now, nearly twenty years later, I find myself embarrassed that our self-
affirming, heterosexual Presbyterian church, for the most part, remains
unrepentant, and that books like this are needed.

Another defining moment in my awakening came the next year with
the abrupt and rude dismissal of Janie Spahr as executive director of our
Council of Oakland Presbyterian Churches (COPC), the unifying arm of
our ten congregations. Before coming to us in the summer of '79, Janie had
graduated from San Francisco Theological Seminary and served three
years as an assistant pastor at First Presbyterian Church, San Rafael,
across the bay. I had hoped we would get someone who had more experience and specific training in community organizing, but everyone else
seemed thrilled with the choice. And when both her spirit and her people
skills immediately became evident, I was quickly and happily converted.

Then, a few months later, in the season when we sing "O Come, O
Come, Emanuel, and ransom captive Israel," she revealed to someone in
one of the churches that her partner, with whom she lived as a couple, was

a woman. Although she made this revelation rather matter-of-factly, the roof of the council fell in. Most of the clergy and elder commissioners went into shock or outrage.

Some, including a few who had been her most avid supporters, wanted to punish her for not telling us ahead of time that she was a lesbian. A few of us appealed to reason but to no avail. We talked about the opportunity to serve the large homosexual community in Oakland and break new ground for our denomination, but our ideas fell on deaf ears. As we braced for Christmas, we asked that at least we do nothing rash. A strong majority, however, decided rash was right. The answer was clear: Homosexual relations are intolerable; there is no room in the inn; and at the first of the year Janie must go. Indeed, with no place to go, with her professional career captive to the council's fear and without its blessing, she went. It was an unmerry Christmas and a sad way to start the '80s.

The ignorance and irrationality that marked the dialogue around Janie did not shock me. As with General Assembly's decision the year before, however, I found myself deeply disappointed. For all of our supposedly sophisticated views of the gospel, we trashed a faithful servant of the church and self-destructed. Some of us tried to keep the council going for the sake of urban mission and congregational support, but too many of the ten churches dropped out. Longtime friendships suffered serious wounds, the scars of which can still be seen. For all practical purposes, fear and hatred backfired on the COPC, and it never really recovered.

In the early '80s, I read a stunning list of history's noted homosexual persons. It was a thought-provoking Who's Who of artists, including many of the greatest masters of all time. I began to ponder three things: First, what would the world be like without these people and many others like them? I thought of the visual beauty, color, music, interpretation, flair, glamour, passion, and pizzazz we all would be missing were it not for their gifts.

Second, because we thwart the creative juices of gays and lesbians in our Presbyterian family, how much have we lost and what do we yet have to lose, we who are known for the color beige, watered-down grape juice, and a black-robed clergy—the church whose leadership some have seen as mainly *male, pale, and stale*? And what can be done to change this?

Third, I had experienced the responses of homosexual persons in the church to be awe-inspiring. Since I began listening to their stories, I found myself nurtured and challenged. In contrast to our church's dark condemnations, their patient testimonies shone like stars in a midnight sky. Against supercilious speeches thrown at them as stones from the self-righteous right, they offered their humble responses to the church as genuine gems, gracious gifts of which it has not been worthy. I began to realize that these servants of Christ were teaching me. And I was increasingly humbled and proud to associate with them.

At the same time, our denomination's treatment of gays and lesbians became more and more important not only to me but also to the Montclair church family. We felt more and more in debt to them and were determined not to let them suffer alone. Since the mid-'70s, they had been making marvelous contributions to our life, serving on committees, the session, and staff. With the 1978 General Assembly decision, the session set up a Gay/Lesbian Concerns Committee and established contact with national Presbyterians for Lesbian and Gay Concerns (PLGC). After acting like a More Light church for a decade, in 1988, the session made its witness formal. In 1995, to evoke the informed dialogue about gays and lesbians to which the 1993 General Assembly called us all, Lisa Larges, of San Francisco, organized *Witness for Reconciliation,* a dramatic presentation of personal stories, mostly focused on coming out. Several lesbian, gay, and straight Montclair members participated, and the session authorized hours for our Associate in Drama, Sally Juarez, to coach the cast. In Albuquerque, at the 1996 General Assembly, after a year of performances in Bay Area churches, the troupe presented its poignant set of stories to a gathering sponsored by PLGC.

It has been empowering to see sessions and congregations as well as individuals develop a sense of being *called out with.* Is it possible that such commitments offer a clue to this present time? Perhaps it is what God had in mind for us all along. Were we more faithful before 1978 than we are in the '90s? Are gays and lesbians less able now than then to help create a more authentic church? Is their oppression in the church any more degrading today than when we assigned them to the church's dark closets?

It was in the mid '80s that I began to become better acquainted with Presbyterian gays and lesbians. Some were out, some were not, but whatever their case, knowing them increased my sympathy to their plight and generated a deeper sense of being *called out with* them. Indeed, our denomination's attitude toward homosexuality has been changing because more of them have been able to let people see them as human beings and support their pursuit of liberation. Of course, when homosexual people come out, some straight church people recoil in fear—as in the case with Janie—and everyone suffers. But others find their testimonies compelling and, in a new birth of openness, throw their arms around them. When that happens, *grace* kicks up her heels. And in W. H. Auden's words, "If there when grace dances, I should dance."

Seeing such evidence of grace, I began to dance more. And while I had long spoken on behalf of God's unconditional love, a gospel that is *exclu-sively inclusive,* and a nonjudgmental Christian ethic, I began to beat the drum more loudly and incessantly for others to dance. In the mid '80s, I wrote an essay titled "One of These Days." I noted that our denomination, having been faced with its racism and sexism, had altered its practices. Just so, I argued, one glorious day the gospel will break the back of its ho-mophobia, freeing it to grant homosexual people all the opportunities of full membership. The piece floated around the Bay Area until 1990, when the Ministry of Light in nearby Marin County began to distribute it na-tionwide. The prophecy, of course, remains unfulfilled. Moreover, many of us may never see that day. This vision, however, remains one impor-tant power that nourishes my hope, drives away discouragement, and draws me to stand with self-affirming, Presbyterian homosexuals.

Another power is my indignation. In 1991, *Sequoia,* an interfaith maga-zine based in Northern California, published another piece I wrote about how the church treats gays and lesbians, titled "Let the Truth Be Known." I asked readers to see that even as the church unknowingly has admired its closeted homosexuals for their devoted service to Christ, it

- remains mostly ignorant of and refuses to learn about ho-mosexuality;
- continues to ignore the 1978 General Assembly directive to fight homophobia in its midst;
- says it hates the sin and loves the sinner while bashing the sinner;
- tolerates anachronistic, biased Bible interpretations that de-mean homosexuals;
- leads the world in hating, oppressing, and persecuting them.

The fact that these disconcerting truths maintain their hold both angers and embarrasses me. It also reminds me that even in formal retirement, I continue to be *called out with.*

Just a year or two ago I read a statement by one of our more conserva-tive theologians to her constituency. She told them, in a stab at appearing gracious, that they must not judge their homosexual brothers and sisters in Christ *too harshly.* I remember thinking, "I thought we weren't to judge one another at all." I also said to myself, "How can we tolerate a church that tolerates discrimination of any kind?" Her words drove me to reaf-firm that Jesus was narrow-minded about broad-mindedness, that he strongly insisted on inclusiveness, that he faithfully battled the judgmen-tal spirit of the Pharisees and of his disciples. If there is anything clear from the biblical record about the loving Christ, it is that we have no right—no moral, ethical, biblical right whatsoever—to patronize, demean, discriminate against, or reject people, including people of faith, who find themselves with sexual orientations different from ours.

Our Presbyterian Church (U.S.A.) continues to pay for its insulting exclusiveness, its insidious acceptance of selective, self-righteous interpretations of the Bible, and its invidious catering to the homophobic biases of the world. It also is paying dearly for asking compassionate Christians to be unfaithful to the loving spirit of the Christ. Every day it

- loses the rich gifts of ministry of its gay and lesbian members;
- drives thoughtful heterosexuals out of its doors by letting its revulsion to homosexuals write its theology and policy;
- sows fear and hatred in its less sophisticated and more insecure members, turning itself into a small-minded, toxic denomination.

The church's behavior will continue to take these terrible tolls. So this book challenges all of us to bear the burden of speaking truth to the Presbyterian Church—as readers of these pages we are all either *called out* or *called out with*. We may merely want to pray, *God save the Church!* But in these days, these terms define something central to the mission of every one of us who identifies with the Christ through the Presbyterian Church.

Faced with this mission, we need not be discouraged. Indeed, one day this church will enter that reign of God under which it will treat gays, lesbians, and, yes, bisexuals and transgendered persons with dignity. *And when we do—on that day, I do believe, the stars will dance, trees will clap their hands, a new day will dawn, and the gospel will give birth to an integrity and joy we have never known before.*

✦ Duke Robinson is an author who lives in Oakland, California, with his spouse, Barbara. They have four children and eight grandchildren. For twenty-eight years before he took early retirement in June of 1996, he served as pastor of the Montclair Presbyterian Church of Oakland, a More Light congregation. Duke's book, *Good Intentions: The Nine Unconscious Mistakes of Nice People,* will be published by Warner Books in the summer of 1997.

7

Love, Sex, and God

✦ ARNOLD B. COME

No human beings have ever been more dearly loved than our two sons, Betty's and mine. They are Bruce and Mac (better known as Lee McClure in the music world of New York). They are of course utterly different, each unique beyond knowing, let alone description. But Bruce was born first, and part of his uniqueness was that in birth he was lost to us (oh, the pain of heart and anguish of spirit!) and then miraculously (to us, way back there in 1944) saved by Caesarian section. And there he was, the happy, laughing, gregarious extrovert from the moment we first held him in our arms. And as he grew up and entered college, his life was full of grand dreams and of great promise.

Then in the middle of his senior year these dreams collapsed. He called us to say he was coming home for Christmas break a few days early. Since Betty and her mother were readying the house for the holiday season, I picked up Bruce at the airport. He was uncharacteristically quiet and tense on the ride home, and as we stopped in the driveway, he said he had something to tell me. He said that he had been having some strange and very disturbing feelings during the last months, feelings of sexual arousal when looking at other men, and he did not know what to do about it. "Dad," he cried out, "I don't want this! I want to get married and have children!" After a moment of silence, I told him: "Bruce, your mother and I will love you no matter what. But if this is your desire, I have heard that one can get counseling to help you move in a different direction. We will help you in any and every way possible." We went into the kitchen where Betty was preparing dinner. She took one look at us and, with her usual profound intuitive insight, said, "What's the matter?" So I told her what Bruce had told me, and she instantly rushed to embrace him, with tears flowing freely, and cried out, "It doesn't matter at all, Bruce! We love you just the way you are."

Of course, these were not our exact words (that was thirty years ago!), but they are an accurate expression of our essential and profoundly held feelings and convictions. Inwardly, Betty and I also experienced a flood of conflicting emotions: numb unbelieving, bewildered confusion, fearful premonitions, a silent hope that it might all go away. But these did not touch or modify in any way our profound love for Bruce and an unquestioning commitment to our bond of devotion.

And so began a long odyssey of self-discovery for all three of us. Bruce returned to college and, with the help of the dean's office, found a psychiatrist who believed that he could redirect Bruce's "sexual preference." From several conversations with the doctor and from reading various articles in medical writings, Betty and I were convinced that Bruce's "problem" was all our fault—which seemed to be the general view in the late 1960s. Full of guilt, we discussed the issue, and each of us claimed full responsibility: the overly busy, neglectful father, and the overly fond and loving mother. In the meantime, Bruce was trying his best to understand his "problem" under the tutelage of the psychiatrist and to establish "normal" behavior with a female companion. After some months of this procedure, he came home in utter despair and despondency. "I just can't make it work," he said.

So I consulted a psychologist friend of mine, and he recommended a psychiatrist at the University of California Medical Center in San Francisco. After a few sessions with him, Bruce's spirit began to lighten and his visage began to brighten, and so I asked him if he would like to tell me what tack this doctor was taking. "It's very simple," he said. "He tells me, 'Bruce, just be yourself. Think and feel and do what is natural to your own being.' What a relief! To believe in myself and to be myself!" "And what does that mean?" I asked. "I simply enjoy the company of men when it comes to sex." "And what about marriage and children?" I asked. "I simply have to accept the fact that that is not for me, to live with and be happy in it," he replied. "But your mother and I feel so guilty about it," I said. "Oh no!" he insisted. "You had nothing to do with it. There is no psychological explanation. It is not a sickness or aberration. It's just the way I am made."

So all three of us went forward on that premise, although it was some time before Betty and I were fully persuaded of it. Across the next few years, Bruce got a job in San Francisco, joined the gay community, and worked to promote understanding and support for their way of life and their civil rights. Betty and I marched with Bruce in parades, went to meetings of their speakers' bureau, got to know both gay and lesbian couples, were invited to his friends' homes for dinners and parties, came to know them as persons, listened to the sad stories of how many of them had been thrown out and disowned by their parents, learned about their presence and success in all walks of life and kinds of employment and their experiences of discrimination when their sexual identity became known. But from that day forward, Bruce insisted on being honest about his sexual identity not only with himself but also in every human relationship. Either people would accept him gladly for who he is in every respect including the sexual, or that relationship would be at an end.

These events have had and continue to have profound effects on me, both personally and professionally. Professionally I am an acknowledged theologian of the Presbyterian Church (U.S.A.), having been ordained as a Presbyterian minister in 1942, teaching in the department of religion of one of our Presbyterian colleges for six years and serving as a professor of systematic theology for thirty years in one of our official Presbyterian seminaries, called on to resource many a committee and commission of General Assembly including the committee that composed the Confession of 1967, writing four theological books published by Westminster Press that have been widely used as resources by both clergy and laity, and still invited in retirement (1982) to staff an occasional committee or to make an address to the General Assembly. How then has my very personal involvement with Bruce and his life as a gay person affected my theological reflections and convictions?

I, like most Presbyterians, had grown up assuming that every human being is either a male or a female and that "sex" had only to do with what happened between them. I was only dimly aware of obscure, usually humorous references to effeminate men as "fairies." I had never known (I thought) one of these rare aberrations. Later in my historical studies I ran across brief references to something called "homosexuality" in ancient Israel and Greece, and in my literary studies I learned about a certain "scandal" attached to Oscar Wilde. I had even heard rumors that a certain college professor was "that," but was uninterested in exploring what "that" actually involved. But then with Bruce, I was suddenly plunged into the need to understand it, both personally and intellectually, and of course theologically. And it happened for me in the midst of all the other revolutions of the '60s and early '70s: civil rights, racial equality, sexual freedom (hetero- of course), political radicalism, invasion of Asian religions into American awareness, the ecumenical movement among the churches, student participation in the governance of higher education, women's rights and women's ordination, and finally war and peace—with the threat of nuclear destruction of the world. All of this involvement was intensified for me when in 1967 I was made president of the Presbyterian seminary where I taught. Now in 1996, I have spent the past fourteen years of so-called retirement in writing a thousand pages (in two volumes) about

Kierkegaard's biblical-Christian understanding of the self, and one major focus has been the nature of love, with the knottiest problem being the relationship between spiritual and sexual love.

What, then, have I come to know and to understand and to believe about love and sex—and God? Two major things. First, for almost every one of us, sexuality is a driving, imperious force that colors everything we do and every relationship we have with other persons. We cannot ignore it but must come to terms with it, because it can be a force either for great good and beauty or for unbelievable degradation and ugliness. Secondly, when it finds its proper function in balance with the totality of the human spirit, it loses its place of primary concern and even becomes a matter for lightness and amusement.

Let me be forthright about one thing. Betty and I are about as *hetero-*sexual as a man and a woman can be. So, without doubt, the profound complementarity of our sexuality had much to do with the powerful magnetic attraction that Betty and I initially felt for each other when we first met at the age of sixteen. Yet at the same time, I was enchanted by the lightness and playfulness of her essential being—she *laughed* at everything I said, and no other girl had ever done that. I was a very intense and serious young man! And she apparently found something attractive about my intense seriousness, which bemused and befuddled me.

But if we thought or spoke at that time about "loving" each other, we could not have separated or distinguished that love from our powerful sexual desire for each other. And throughout fifty-four years of marriage, we have gradually learned how to enjoy and to share our sexual/gender identities with each other. I have learned and treasured and unconsciously absorbed into my self something of that mysterious identity called "femininity," and she has been opened up to and been intrigued by what my "maleness" has been able to offer to our common life. But one thing I have learned from association with the gay/lesbian community: it is hopeless to try to define these terms that so clearly distinguish between a man and a woman.

Quite to the contrary of this magnetic sexual attraction that bound us together, there gradually emerged, in the process of our sixty-plus years of intimate companionship, another totally different and clearly distinguishable dimension in our loving relationship. Sexual attraction *by itself* proves to be a shifting, unstable, unreliable ground for a continuing relationship. The dream of perfection in actual sexual intercourse, as projected in some romantic literature and especially in movies, turns out to be false, a luring but deceptive illusion. But we learned to accept this imperfection without rancor or bitterness or disillusionment because gradually, through the intimacy of marriage and of parenthood, we came to see and to know and to embrace the identity of each other as a human being, a person, a self, created in the image of God; and *as such,* we know each other as totally equal, precisely the same in dignity and worth, in a way that completely transcends our gender differentiation and our sexual relationship. And from this perspective, all sexuality and sexual activity take on a lightness and even a humorous quality. And yet our continuing sexual relationship, while serving as a pleasurable satisfaction of a physical desire, also miraculously serves as the occasion and the medium of an unparalleled intimacy of spirit.

All this was developing precisely along with and in relation to my own personal struggle to understand homosexuality during the 1960s and '70s. The interaction of these two absorptions of my mind and spirit have led me to certain undeniable insights and firm convictions.

One's sexuality, whatever kind or degree, does not define in any way an individual's identity as person/self/spirit. In other words, the "image of God" in which each of us human beings is created has nothing to do with God's act of also creating us "male and female" (Genesis 1:27). The latter simply identifies us with the rest of the "animal" world in our means of reproduction. Yet they cannot be separated into separate compartments of our lives. Sexual relationships undoubtedly pose one of the severest tests and also one of the most glorious occasions for realization of the ideal of always relating to another human being out of respect and concern for the other's spiritual identity as person or self. And yet one does not have to be related to another human being sexually at all in order to fulfill one's potentiality of becoming a person/self in the image of God. Many of the most profoundly spiritual persons throughout history have remained celibate (for one reason or another) all their lives. It is also true that gay men, including Bruce, often develop close friendships with heterosexual women, and I am sure that lesbian women do the same with heterosexual men. And certainly the female partner of a sexual relationship does not have to be subservient to the male in order to relate to God—the apostle Paul to the contrary (see Ephesians 5:21–32; 1 Corinthians 14:34–35).

So I became convinced that gays and lesbians who seek and gladly accept the guidance of the Spirit of God in the whole of their lives should be welcomed into the full communion of the church's life, including of course leadership roles. From my own personal knowledge of and friendship with them, I know that their sexuality *as such* is no more of a barrier to becoming full and rich human spirits in the image of God than is my own sexuality. Indeed, I know that my son Bruce and many of his gay and lesbian friends are highly principled, morally concerned, kind and compassionate in all their personal relationships. Many of them are as committed to helping the poor, the lonely, the oppressed, the mentally or physically impaired as any Christians I know. For many years, Bruce was a highly valued counselor on an emergency talk-line for parents, both men and women, who felt they were in danger of abusing their children. Every week he would give a whole night or a Saturday/Sunday to be ready for those calls, ready to go in the middle of the night to carry a baby to a shelter away from a drunken or deranged parent. And in recent years I have come to know an increasing number of the gays and lesbians who are already serving as very effective and highly valued ministers in the Presbyterian church.

In other words, sexuality is a secondary quality of human nature, and not to be taken with primary seriousness when judging the true character and identity of a human being. And every sexual act between any two human beings reflects our human propensity to failure, and every sexual act needs compassionate understanding and indulgence (as well as a sense of humor!) from both a loving God and a patient partner. So I have always felt compassionately accepting of divorced and remarried couples, even though Jesus bluntly asserted that they commit adultery every time they have intercourse (Mark 10:11–12), because, after all, Jesus also said that "everyone who looks at a woman lustfully has already committed adultery with her in his heart" (Matthew 5:28). Let me say it again: when it comes to engaging in sexual activity, all of us, male and female, heterosexual and homosexual, equally need compassion, indulgence, and especially a sense of *humor,* one toward the other.

One final perspective on sexuality, love, and God, that I have come to over these years. I have read and contemplated many times all the passages of scripture, both Jewish and Christian, that condemn homosexual relations. I have especially thought through Paul's contention that those relations are "contrary to nature" (*para physin* in Greek). Note: he does not say "contrary to the law of God" or "contrary to the teachings of Jesus Christ." And this is an important distinction for Paul himself, as he makes clear in his letters to the church in Corinth. In discussing diverse problems of marriage, sometimes he says that "*not* I but the *Lord*" makes a certain demand, but more often he says that "to the rest *I* say, *not* the Lord," or "I have no command of the Lord, but I give *my* opinion," or "in *my* judgment" a widow "is happier if she stays as she is" but adds uncertainly, "I *think* that I have the spirit of God" (1 Corinthians 7:10, 12, 25, 40). And even when he says that "*nature* itself teach[es] that for a man to wear long hair is degrading" but for a woman "it is her pride," he admits that he is only talking about the "practice" that is generally recognized by the churches (1 Corinthians 11:13–16).

So, then, what Paul means by the category of "nature" is not completely clear, but it is clear that Paul is not thinking about, nor seems at all aware of, an inborn homosexual nature as we have experienced and become informed about in the late nineteenth and twentieth centuries. In our contemporary church, biblical scholars would appear to conceive of nature in much broader categories than Paul. For a faith grounded in the whole Bible, nature is God's creation in which God has set the human species to develop its own unique form of life. As our own Presbyterian Confession of 1967 says, "God has created the world of space and time to be the sphere of [God's] dealings with [human beings]. In its beauty and vastness, sublimity and awfulness, order and disorder, the world reflects to the eye of faith the majesty and mystery of its Creator" (9:16, i.e., Part I, Section B, § 2).

As someone has said, "nature's imagination is richer than ours," leaving us to marvel at its manifold diversity of forms of life, as well as its unfathomable structures and dynamics. Naturalists tell us—and now we *see* it on television—that homosexual relations occur throughout the animal kingdom, at least from insects on up. And now anthropologists and psychologists tell us that sexuality among human beings shares in that rich diversity of nature in general. Pure, total homosexuality and pure, total heterosexuality are extremes on a spectrum that reveals infinite variations, and I have come to know both gay and lesbian individuals who find themselves bewildered by their ability and even desire to live, at times, toward both ends of the spectrum. No one *chooses* where she or he is given to be in this variety. I did not choose to be heterosexual and Bruce did not choose to be homosexual, and neither of us can *un*choose or refuse what we have been given to be. It is a given of life. Furthermore, each individual human self, with its unique DNA, manifests its own given sexual drive in its own personal way. No wonder none of the romantic icons or types in novels and movies ever fit the actual situation of a real individual!

And all this is God's good creation. But it is not nature that determines the goodness or evil, the beauty or ugliness, of human behavior and life. It only sets the stage and does require each of us to *choose* what we will make of what we have been given. And in our freedom to create beauty or ugliness, we all need the help of loving, compassionate, understanding parents and/or friends. Ultimately, we need to turn to the Source and Giver of Life in order to find the Way to the Truth that sets us free to come into the fullness of the image of God, of the infinite and eternal dignity and worth, that resides in the hidden depths of every single human being.

We must remember, every day and every hour, that once we *all* were "strangers to the covenants of promise, having no hope and without God in the world" (Ephesians 2:11–14). But this "wall of hostility" was broken down and we were welcomed into the "peace" of God's loving-kindness. The one and only deed required of every follower of Jesus the Christ is this: to welcome *every* seeker of the way to a life out of the storm of this world's hopelessness and hostility, no matter how "strange" that seeker may seem to be, to embrace that seeker in the arms of God's love and then—leave it to God to guide that seeker to the Truth. Please, please, my fellow Christians/Presbyterians, listen to these words, take them into your heart, and *do* them, this day, this hour.

⇥ Arnold B. Come is Professor Emeritus of San Francisco Theological Seminary and the Graduate Theological Union and President Emeritus of San Francisco Theological Seminary.

8

God's *Life* Style:
No Strangers

✦ PEG BEISSERT

I wear a button marked "honorary lesbian." When I was so named after my term as interim minister at heavily gay West Hollywood Presbyterian Church, I joined in the laughter. But as time went by, in which I directed the justice-seeking Lazarus Project in Southern California, I gained a different perspective. For me, it is now an honor to wear the button. I treasure it because it identifies who I am, a solid supporter of gays and lesbians. And it means I am included with and by these friends.

In my work for the Lazarus Project (a ministry that works against the bigotry of church and society toward such persons) I have told audiences, "Wherever you are on this issue, I've been there . . . all the way from total ignorance to full respect and outrage over the deprivation and denigration of this part of God's family." What happened? God led me into situations where I had opportunities to learn to appreciate gay men and lesbians as persons. We are no longer strangers.

My journey began when I was in seminary, very near the end of my studies. In an adult therapy group, a man I thought had everything going for him for ministry told us he was gay. He was intelligent, caring, warm and witty, knowledgeable, committed. I told myself, "This is impossible. Not Jack. He does not fit my picture of a gay man."

Obviously, I had an inaccurate stereotype in my head. The picture society had given me of gay men . . . all fluff, no substance . . . was all wrong. I had a lot of adjusting to do!

It was only a short time later following graduation from Drew Seminary and work at Christ Church in Summit, New Jersey, that I was called to a church in California and was placed on the Candidates Committee of Pacific Presbytery. This was exciting at times when highly eligible candidates for the ministry came before us, persons you trusted to serve Jesus Christ with vigor and vision. There were other times when you worried about what the church might become.

Toward the end of my six-year term, the chair told us that an openly gay man would be present at our next meeting. Some had heard of Chris

Glaser; I did not know him. I arrived to find Chris, a Yale Divinity School graduate, saying, "I want to be honest about who I am." There was something tremendously appealing about this honesty as he looked directly at each of us. His academic responses were immediate and correct. There was no doubt about his understanding of Reformed theology. The more we questioned, the more certain I became this man was head and shoulders over any candidate I had met.

I admit I fought for him in that committee "like a tiger." We passed him with a 7-to-5 vote. Eventually, of course, the presbytery "crucified" him. Presbytery asked him to conclude the examination by leading us in prayer! I have always remembered that his prayer included support "for those ministers present who are gay!"

After this, I knew I had to do something with my own commitment on this "homosexual" question. My husband, Al, and I talked at great length and I found him very open and supportive of the path that was opening before me.

I was asked by Chris Glaser to preach at West Hollywood Presbyterian Church where he was starting the Lazarus Project. My husband and I entered a new a world, a world in which dedicated Christians—medical doctors, lawyers, teachers, principals, men and women respected in their communities—were mostly living "in the closet" and feeling they must deny publicly who they were. They greeted us with warmth and affection.

This new world offered a church service that is any minister's dream: people attentive, eager, joyous, and present with the deep conviction that they are God's beloved. To preach at West Hollywood means having the congregation "with you" in both serious moments and in laughter. Sunday here is one morning of the week when gay men and lesbians can be free of concern over rejection, can be accepted as lovable people, can be the people who God created them to be. One visitor said, "The whole congregation is a choir."

This is part of the gay world? *This* is what it means to be a *gay* or *lesbian* Christian? The more I preached there, the longer I served as interim pastor, and when I became director of the Lazarus Project, the more the injustice toward gays and lesbians hit me in the face.

I came to see that the Presbyterian church is indeed the sinner, causing loving, upright people to be ashamed God created them. Who are we to limit God's activity? Why may we sit in judgment?

I had a lot of growing to do. Step by step, always ready to answer my questions, never angry with my ignorance, these gay and lesbian

Christians led me into understanding. It helped to have a husband with whom I could speak freely. There are little moments along the way I recall.

We were at a Presbytery dinner. A small group of gay men arrived just after we had been seated. There was a quiet moment as they stood there. Places were available, but a new table was set up for them. "It feels like we're treating them like lepers," I said to my husband. I left to get a cup of coffee. Al was gone when I returned. After a while, I asked those near me if they knew where he was. One man nodded his head toward the "gay" table. I knew then that my husband was "with me" . . . and why I had married him.

Through these past ten years, knowing my own slow progression, I have understood the hesitancy of people to support gays and lesbians. What I have not understood is the depth of hatred and the bitterness some people display. Now as I reflect on all our experiences together, I have an explanation to offer.

There is a basic element in human nature that makes us fearful of the stranger, the one who is different. We see how babies must overcome this fear, how they need time to allow themselves to be held even by grandparents. I assume we inherit this as self-preservation from the animal kingdom.

This is why I come face to face with God in the story of Sodom. Both anti- and pro-gay factions, who are to any extent biblical scholars, now agree the biblical story of Sodom and Gomorrah is not about homosexuality. It is about inhospitality. But this did not satisfy me as the last word. I kept asking myself: *Why* were the Sodomites inhospitable? *Why* were they so mean-spirited?

It came to me as a revelation. What is really exposed in this story is the fear of strangers. The heart of the message is God's anger with the Sodomites for rejecting other human beings. God is saying, "You are all part of my family. I will not tolerate a lack of acceptance of each other."

As a parent and grandparent, I now understand God's joy when members of my family are kind to each other, even partying joyously together. But too often, what have we done? We have distorted God's message, limiting and destroying the lives of our gay and lesbian "relatives." May God forgive us.

It is only when we really step into the gay and lesbian scene that we realize how destructive the church has been in the lives of these people and how much we are harming them. It is a shocking experience for those of us who had no idea of our callousness.

It does demand a leap in attitude for us to change our views. I am thankful that God has allowed me insight as a pastoral counselor to begin to bridge the "stranger" syndrome. It brought me to my senses when I heard different gay and lesbian versions of a repeated sentence: "I was seven when I knew I was different." When I pressed the statement, the answers were similar. Lesbians and gay men often have a sense that the picture of "mom, dad, and the kids" was somehow not in their future. Going back to my years in Christian education, I recall in child development a stage around six or seven when the child first becomes aware of a world beyond the family. There is a branching out, knowing "I am part of a bigger world." And that world often does not fit for the gay or lesbian child.

Another leap in awareness for heterosexuals lies in understanding human sexuality. We are given responsibility for our bodies, and as Christians, we believe whatever we do with our bodies should be done in love. There is something sacred in the offering of one body to another for pleasure and fulfillment. I fail to see that there is only one way for our bodies to pleasure one another, so long as the experience is mutual and in no way destructive.

My ministry has been primarily with gay and lesbian persons, but not exclusively. I have counseled with those who feel they are bisexual and I've had a few conversations with transgendered persons. We are all God's children. When I am asked if I think homosexuality is genetic, my reply is that sexuality is genetic and it comes in a variety of forms. Why is it so difficult for us to appreciate our differences, whether in the homosexual or heterosexual world? Why must we remain strangers to one another?

The church has left gays and lesbians to form their own relationships and committed unions. Denied the rite of marriage, same-gender partners who love each other will find a way to live together and make their own promises to each other. They have discovered that the blessing of the church is not necessary in order to recognize their unions as sacred. But it is still a struggle to obtain civil rights for those unions. It seems only right that gays and lesbians are entitled to the civil benefits of marriage, since they contribute taxes just as heterosexuals do to uphold a protective legal system in our nation. I believe they deserve to have the rite of marriage extended to them by the church.

I continue to be appalled at the derogatory names inflicted on gay and lesbian persons . . . and this *within* our churches. In my presence they have been called "abominations," "heretics," and "perverts." Men have said, "You turn my stomach," and "You disgust me." It hurts beyond words to hear the friends I value treated so despicably. It should be unthinkable to malign brothers and sisters in Christ, mawkishly saying we "love" them, while at the same time maiming their lives and denying God's call to them. How can we possibly say we are Christians? Christians follow the Christ and act in Christ's spirit. Where do we have any evidence of the God-embodied Jesus of Nazareth denigrating, shaming, and belittling another person into nothingness? We all know such demeaning actions by Christians are a sacrilege.

A final story concerns my return from the 1996 Presbyterian General Assembly in Albuquerque. It was there that Presbyterians again denied ordination as ministers, elders, or deacons to self-affirming gays and lesbians.

My homecoming from the Assembly was depressing. That baptized members of our church family had been treated cruelly, had been stripped of their human dignity, and that it had been done in the name of God was more than I could handle. So on the first Sunday after this experience, I drove to West Hollywood Church just to be with my friends.

I left that worship service on top of the world! Very little was said about the Assembly's action. Instead, the service upheld our faith. For gays and lesbians, this is an indomitable faith. They do not fall apart in adversity because they know God walks with them. They are not strangers to God.

That morning, the Rev. Dan Smith's sermon centered on the Hebrew midwives who refused to accept Pharaoh's cruel demands that they kill all newborn Hebrew males. The midwives resisted—and placed themselves between Pharaoh and the unjust slaughter of innocents. When they refused to comply with Pharaoh's fears and orders, the midwives' faith was strengthened and they found the courage to be agents of God's liberating will.

The message seems clear: God's loving justice will prevail despite the sinful arrogance and control designs of the powers that be.

↝ The Rev. Peg Beissert is a former director of the Lazarus Project, a Presbyterian-related organization in Southern California, seeking justice for gay and lesbian Christians. She is on Presbytery of the Pacific staff as editor of the News Bulletin. A widow and mother of three, she has been a journalist and Christian educator. She was ordained as a Presbyterian clergywoman in 1971 and has served churches on both coasts.

9

With Mind and Heart

→ MARY WITHERSPOON

When I was in college some forty years ago, my psychology teacher told us that people's sexual orientation was determined at birth or at a very early age. I recall that this opinion engendered some spirited conversation, which the professor loved so much that I always took his statements with a grain of salt. But in this case, his arguments seemed well-founded and fit with my own observations. It seemed to me then that if one does not choose one's sexual orientation, one should not be condemned if that orientation varies from the norm. As this subject has been explored in more recent years, I have repeatedly tested my early conclusion against scripture, new medical evidence, and my personal experiences with gay and lesbian persons. And I have found no reason to change my conviction.

Although there are passages in scripture that describe homosexual practice as sinful, I believe that these prohibitions were expressed in an age when the understanding and practice of sexuality was different from ours. In pre-Christian Greece, for example, sexual relations between males were common and accepted, and sexual relations were even a part of temple worship. Perhaps the scriptures express early Christian reaction to such practices. As Christians, we understand that it is sinful for a married man or woman to seek sexual fulfillment with someone other than his or her mate. However, it does not follow that the *only* honorable marital relationship has to be that between a man and a woman. And it seems to me to be untenable for Christianity to require that a gay man or a lesbian live a celibate life when an honorable relationship with a person of the same sex can be fulfilling in the same way that a heterosexual relationship can be.

I think that the scripture passages that teach acceptance are more compelling than those that condemn homosexual practice. Jesus said, "Come to me all you that are weary and are carrying heavy burdens, and I will give you rest." Given the rejection by our society of homosexual people—their ostracism, their abuse, the denial of their civil rights—one must conclude that this invitation is surely for them, the heavy-laden. If Paul says that in Christ there is neither male nor female, we can conclude that one's sexual nature does not determine whether one can be a full member of the body of Christ.

As I understand it, medical research has increasingly indicated that sexual preference is predetermined and may indeed be physiological. If this is correct, then it is hard to see how homosexuality can be inherently blameworthy, since it is not under one's control.

My own experiences with gays and lesbians have verified my conviction that same-sex relationships are not necessarily sinful. One of the most poignant conversations I ever had was with a lesbian who told me the story of her courtship with her mate. I had invited this woman to lead sessions on spirituality for a group I was coordinating. We had chosen her because we knew her to be a deeply spiritual person, and she asked me to meet with her before she accepted the invitation. She wanted me to know of her long-term relationship with another woman, so that I would not be embarrassed if this came up. She also wanted me to be free to withdraw the invitation if I thought it was appropriate to do so. I knew that she lived with another woman, although their relationship had never been described precisely to me before this time. I appreciated her candor; it made clear what had been murky. It did not, however, alter my understanding of her as a spiritual person well-suited to lead our sessions.

Another gay couple with whom we have worked is an example of two people who care deeply for each other. Each does small things to make life easier for the other; each is proud of the accomplishments of the other. In short, they have the kind of relationship that most heterosexual couples seek. Nevertheless, one of these men (with whom I've never discussed the issue of homosexuality) once said to me that if he'd had his "druthers," he would rather never have been born. It is tragic that our society would cause such a caring man—who is always buying birthday gifts for his numerous nieces and nephews, who makes sure that repairs are made on his mother's house, who is remarkably unselfish—to view himself in such a way.

My husband has a long-time friend who is gay—a person who cares about others and about whom others care. For many years he was a faithful member of his church, singing in the choir and contributing in many ways. Today that has changed. I do not know whether this is a result of the attitude that churches take toward their gay and lesbian members, but I do not believe that he should be a second-class member of any church, as he would be if he were a Presbyterian. I think that our churches need lesbian and gay members. I have participated in group events with homosexual couples, and I have been aware of an atmosphere of caring, acceptance, and excitement at being together that should characterize the church, but often does not.

It seems inconsistent to me for us to say that we welcome gay and lesbian people into the church, but we will not ordain them. To be a Reformed Christian means that we are "blessed to be a blessing." Can the church then say that one can be a blessing in the choir, in the kitchen, in the classroom, on the landscaping crew, but one can't be a blessing as a deacon (where some of my gay friends belong because they have an extra measure of compassion) or as an elder or pastor? It makes no sense to me! We do not need hierarchies of members.

I think that we need to be clear that to be in favor of full acceptance of gay and lesbian people into the church does not mean that we accept promiscuity. I am turned off by some of the exhibitionism of gays and lesbians that I see on TV. I am even more turned off by Madonna writhing in chains while singing a song on MTV. Neither of these scenes remotely resembles anything with which I am personally familiar. I believe that people of all sexual orientations should make the same kind of commitment to monogamy and to building relationships that honor God and build up one's partner. I don't think that there is a place in the life of a Christian for the kind of selfishness which has, in our society, put one's own gratification above everything else. The gay and lesbian people that I know go about their lives just as many heterosexual people do—working, volunteering, worshiping, and caring for family members.

My strong conviction is that we should accept into the church everyone who seeks to follow Christ, and elect to office and ordain those with exemplary lives whose gifts fit them for the office of elder, deacon, or pastor.

⇥ Mary Witherspoon lives in Huntsville, Alabama, where she is an elder at Covenant Presbyterian Church. She has served as moderator of council of the North Alabama Presbytery, a member of the presbytery Peacemaking Committee, and a member of the program committee of the Huntsville Peace Group. She has been president of Church Women United in Huntsville and vice-chair of the Madison County Democratic Executive Committee. Mary is the wife of Newell Witherspoon and the mother of Joan, Ann, Ed and Hibi, John and Jackie.

➤10➤

It Is the Right Thing to Do

✦ JOSÉ OLAGUES

The Beginning

What an unwieldy task I undertook when I agreed to be a contributor to this volume! When did I become an advocate for my gay, lesbian, bisexual, and transgendered sisters and brothers? I was asked to trace the journey that led to my present stand. How could I do that? It's impossible for me to trace. I have come to equate this question with another very difficult question: When does life begin?

In order to deal with the question, I had to modify it: When did I become an advocate for the disenfranchised or a voice for the voiceless? With my apologies to my sisters and brothers, this modification was necessary for me, not because I do not believe that the topic of being gay, lesbian, bisexual, or transgendered in our society and in our denomination warrants discussion and needs to be dealt with, but because I am convinced that I cannot address the topic without dealing with the broader topic of justice that comes from our Creator God. I just cannot separate it! I am called by God to work for justice, and thus address issues of injustice around me.

Reflecting

As I reflect on my life, I recall numerous advocacy positions I have undertaken, and I am convinced that my childhood upbringing has led me to take those stands. In the adult phase of my life some of the precursor advocacy for voiceless groups includes:

Industry–corporation. During the 1970s my professional job responsibilities included implementation of affirmative-action plans for a major telecommunications company. Successfully placing qualified new employees, particularly those in nontraditional gender roles, required "training" managers in the new paradigms of the time, and recruiting in conjunction with community organizations.

Family–children. I will forever be indebted to Beverly, my wife, and our biological children, Tanya, Khristina, and José Burns, for their willingness to be part of our family's ministry. For eleven years we committed ourselves to opening the doors of our home to children whose biological parents were unable to provide for their safety, abandoned them, and/or abused them physically, mentally, or sexually. Temporarily, 287 troubled children became part of our lives and we in turn became their advocates, including intervening in the court system when their welfare was not the main concern in social service department recommendations. As a result of that ministry, our family grew by the adoption of our two youngest children, Jessika and JayCee.

Church–society. I am convinced that the church cannot afford to separate itself from the society of which it is a part. I have been vocal on the need to empower the powerless, both in the society at large and definitely within the church. For the past two decades, my advocacy in the church has been for not only people of color but youth, the elderly, women, gays and lesbians, non-English speakers, and the physically challenged.

Personal Faith

My upbringing recognized that each of my sisters and brothers was created by our loving Creator, as was I, in the image of God's self and thus we are all children of the same God. I learned that we are all entitled to the love, mercy, and justice that come from our Creator, and that this Creator God blesses us with unique gifts. Obviously influenced by this upbringing, in my personal statement of faith I claim:

> This loving God is still creating, and as the creation continues, not only are we entrusted as stewards of the creation, but God consistently nurtures us like a gentle mother and provides for us like a devoted father. This eternal God while calling us into covenant relationship, claims us and gives each of us particular gifts. This living and eternal God, revealed through scripture, also calls us to be just, and to live our lives in community in service to others.

Injustice in Our Midst

If I recognize that I am called to work for justice, I obviously notice the exclusion of gay, lesbian, bisexual, and transgendered persons from the full life of our denomination. This exclusion is, of course, a gross violation of the principles that govern us. My personal studies have informed my opinion, and I am convinced that there is nothing in the Bible that should prevent anyone from being ordained in our denomination simply because of her or his sexual orientation, when the person is committed to a loving, caring (hetero or homo) relationship. I arrive at this conclusion when I study the original texts, so often cited by those who disagree with my opinion, without the lenses of systematic theology. Too often it is the theologians' presuppositions, and not theology itself, that determines interpretation; or if it is theology, it is a dogmatic expression carried from the second century which attempts consistency with itself without regard to the reality of our contemporary situation. (See L. William Countryman, *Dirt, Greed, and Sex* [Philadelphia: Fortress Press, 1990], 3.)

Resulting Damage

I have been blessed to know and to work with incredibly gifted gay and lesbian persons both within and outside the church. But as I have become aware of the stories of rejection of these wonderfully gifted persons who have been committed to our denomination, I am pained. I am the proud owner of the first "officially" sold copy of *Called Out*, and I know that I wept as I read the stories, particularly that of my friend Melinda McLain. Although born a Presbyterian, she despaired of the ability of our denomination to afford the justice she sought and found a call in the United Church of Christ. Rev. Melinda, I love you, and I was glad to rejoice with you as another part of the Christian family recognized your talents, gifts, and call. Alleluia! I am ashamed for the Presbyterian Church (U.S.A.). Has legalism made us into slaves? Have we forgotten that Jesus still calls us to feed the hungry, clothe the naked, comfort the afflicted, and bring the good news to the world?

I was overcome by emotions following the vote that continues the ban on ordination of gays and lesbians by the 208th General Assembly in Albuquerque in 1996. I joined the ranks of seven to eight hundred to express grief over the vote, and I wept once more. I wept because of the pain of having to tell my sisters and brothers that our denomination has voted, one more time, to continue abusing them. What happened to the gospel of love? Have we become the legalistic church that Christ wanted to get rid of? How long, O God, how long?

Recurring Topic

In a recent conversation with Beverly, my wife, the topic came up again, and as I find myself seeking a new call, she asked, " . . . but why do you *always* have to be on the side of the voiceless? . . . refugees, children, oppressed, gays and lesbians?" In at least one case, after I preached before the search committee in a neutral pulpit, my position on the issue of ordination, articulated just before the 208th General Assembly, contributed to my receiving a "rejection" letter. I obviously cannot answer her question, which in essence is the same question raised by the editors of this volume, without relating it to my spiritual-religious formation. I simply have to say that I do it because it is the right thing to do; I do it because I am called to do so, if I am to consider myself a disciple of Christ.

A lectionary passage of the Hebrew scripture that traditionally has been troublesome for me recently spoke to me on this issue. I was using the text as I preached at Stone Presbyterian Church of Willow Glen–San José. I related one of my earliest recollections as the oldest of three brothers (José, Reuben, Benjamin) in a household with significant Hebrew family influence. I was envious (covetous?) of my younger brother when he received a gift of long pants from a neighbor. I was five years old and growing in very tropical Mazatlán, Mexico. Like many children of my age, I wore shorts all year long, and I did not own a pair of long pants until later. There were no plots to kill, and I don't remember, at that time, any of the three brothers taking a stand to save one another, but I am still troubled, almost half a century later, whenever I encounter the story.

The Sermon: "Reuben's Beautiful Feet"
Genesis 37:1–4, 12–28

Joseph is one of the younger brothers and his father's favorite son. He had a special coat that his father had made for him (vv. 1–4). He is sent by his father, Jacob, to inquire about the older brothers who are shepherding away from home (v. 14), and as the young shepherd catches up with them

(vv. 14–17), we find a plot to get rid of him, the one they dislike (vv. 18–20). It is here that those shepherd feet of Reuben, the eldest of them, take a stand (read vv. 21–22). There is more to the story: Joseph eventually ends up in Egypt (v. 28).

Reflect on that part of the story (vv. 21–22) where we find Reuben taking a stand and making a difference. We need to ask the questions, Why did he speak up for his younger brother? After all, didn't Joseph deserve to die? He was not only a dreamer, he was Papa's favorite son! If they were to get rid of him, wouldn't things be more equitable? We do know that Reuben was the eldest, and some concern for the welfare of his younger brother is expected of him.

But didn't Reuben realize that he was putting himself in jeopardy? Could he not see that, by standing up, he could have been the one killed? What was the matter with Reuben—was he mad? Was he crazy? Some might claim that he was.

I have come to realize that we can find a number of other characters in the Bible who in their time and place were considered "crazy." This label is often used when a particular group sees things from a perspective that differs from that of another group or individual. Read Matthew 3:1–4 and Luke 3:7–9. By today's standards, if we were to meet John the Baptist, I'm almost sure that we would consider him "mad" or "crazy."

Many of the prophets would certainly be worthy of the same label. Elisha, Jeremiah, Hosea, and a host of others were likely labeled as being mad and were probably considered demented. And they were found guilty.

But what were they guilty of? Well, they did engage in unusual and strange activities. They were calling the leadership, including kings, to task. They were calling them to account for injustice that was occurring around them. Imagine that! The audacity of them to question the king! Who did they think they were, anyway?

Robert McAfee Brown, in *Saying Yes and Saying No: On Rendering to God and Caesar* (Philadelphia: Westminster Press, 1986), argues that there are times when we must separate ourselves from a portion of our contemporaries, from parts of our society, from our leadership, and even from our government in order to give an unqualified *yes* to God and an unqualified *no* to injustice. Brown calls it a blasphemy when we talk about God but do not notice injustice around us. He also deals with some of the creative "excuses" we use as crutches to avoid taking a stand: not having enough information; having enough information to know that the issue is too complex; the time is not yet right.

In one of Brown's chapters we are introduced to Abraham Joshua Heschel as someone who exemplified the prophetic tradition, someone raised by God to speak to us in the twentieth century. For a long time and until his death in 1972 Heschel was professor of ethics and mysticism at the Jewish Theological Seminary of America. I was struck by the illustration at the closing of the chapter from Heschel's own life, dealing with the excuse of not speaking until the "right time" comes.

Brown explains that both he and Heschel were present at a meeting in Washington, D.C., in 1967. Heschel, who spoke immediately before Brown, already feared that people of conscience would not speak against the Vietnam involvement until it was too late, and he recounted some of his boyhood fears. We find Heschel in Poland when he, with a rabbi, is studying the Torah, at the age of seven. Together they were reading the story of the sacrifice of Isaac, the Akeda. Brown tells us of Heschel's recounting:

> Isaac was on the way to Mount Moriah with his father; then he lay on the altar, bound, waiting to be sacrificed. My heart began to beat even faster; it actually sobbed with pity for Isaac. Behold Abraham now lifted the knife. And now my heart froze within me with fright. Suddenly the voice of the angel was heard: "Abraham, lay not thine hand upon the lad, for now I know that thou fearest God."
>
> And here I broke into tears and wept aloud. "Why are you crying?" asked the rabbi. "You know Isaac was not killed."
>
> And I said to him, still weeping, "But Rabbi, supposing the angel had come a second too late?"
>
> The rabbi comforted me, and calmed me by telling me that an angel cannot come too late.

Brown continues: "And then, lifting his eyes from his manuscript and looking directly into our eyes, Heschel concluded: 'An angel cannot come too late, my friends, but we, made of flesh and blood, we may come too late.'" (From Abraham Joshua Heschel, *Vietnam: Crisis of Conscience* [New York: Association Press, 1967], 51–52, slightly altered in Robert McAfee Brown, *Saying Yes and Saying No*, 56.)

These two stories—Reuben's stand, and Heschel's admonition not to wait too long—keep bringing to my mind the present impasse in our denomination. The question of whether to ordain our lesbian sisters and gay brothers has brought a lack of conversation and physical, literal, theological, spiritual, distance between the most conservative and most liberal members. I have come to believe that this issue is even broader. I believe this issue comes to the simple acceptance of lesbian, gay, bisexual, and transgendered individuals in our congregations and denomination.

As Christians, we are called to become prophets and to address issues of injustice. We are indeed called to say *yes* to our Creator God and *no* to injustice even within our own denomination.

Like Reuben, we need to speak up and take a stand, while keeping everyone in the family. Taking a lesson from Abraham Joshua Heschel, we must also exercise caution that we do not wait too long before we take a stand (or act up). If we delay unnecessarily, we may come to the table too late. Amen.

❖ After twenty-one years in the corporate world, and with extensive lay leadership experience in the Presbyterian Church, particularly in the area of racial ethnic ministries, José Olagues received a master of divinity degree from San Francisco Theological Seminary in May 1995. Until late 1996 he served as interim associate executive presbyter for program for San Jose Presbytery. While in seminary, he also served in youth ministries positions at First Presbyterian Church–San Rafael, California, and at Calvary Presbyterian Church–San Francisco. José and his wife, Beverly, have been married for more than thirty years, and their family includes five children (ranging in age from eleven to twenty-eight) and a three-year-old grandchild.

11

A Journey in Understanding

❧ LILLIAN McCULLOCH TAYLOR

Sexuality was seldom discussed in the Southern home and community into which I was born more than sixty years ago. And terms specifying differing categories of sexuality were never mentioned there at all. So it was not until I was a young adult that the words "homosexual" and "heterosexual" had any specific meaning for me. Indeed, I recall saying to my pastor-husband, while we were both still in our twenties, "I don't know anyone who is a homosexual." To which he replied, "Oh yes you do!" Later, when we had moved away from that parish to another, he felt free to name those in that first congregation whom we had together known and loved, persons whom he knew to have been wrestling with their own sexual identity. That was forty years ago. In the next two decades, I had little occasion to face the question again, though my thoughts have often returned to those early and cherished parishioners of whose intimate identity I had been so little aware.

In the meantime, I became a lover of books. My journey, both into feminism and into openness toward and support for persons of differing sexual orientation, has been initiated and nurtured through books. Authors are living people who are able to lay bare their minds and souls in print.

It was through a book, *Women, Men, and the Bible,* that I first encountered the strong voice of Virginia Ramey Mollenkott, and it affected me deeply. The book is not about sexuality, but it *is* about gender; and it started me on the long road to becoming a Christian feminist. Later on, this same author would illuminate my understanding of human sexuality. I came to know her as a friend.

In 1985 my husband and I attended together the meeting of the General Assembly of the Presbyterian Church (U.S.A.) held in Indianapolis. We noted on the Assembly program that Virginia Mollenkott was scheduled to be the principal speaker at a luncheon meeting of the group called "Presbyterians for Lesbian and Gay Concerns" (or PLGC, as it is commonly known), an independent advocacy group within the denomination. Delighted at the opportunity to hear her again, we immediately bought tickets for the PLGC luncheon and attended the meeting. She spoke movingly of the plight of lesbian and gay persons in the church today; and for the first time, in that connection, she used the pronoun, "we." That was all—but the point was not lost on the attendees. It was her "coming out" as a lesbian Christian, and in the question-and-answer period that followed, she spoke openly of her sexual orientation.

Speaking privately with Virginia after the meeting, I expressed to her my total surprise at her announcement. She responded that it had taken her this long to "come out" because, as she said, "I was always taught to think that this was dirty, and so from childhood I was taught to hide these feelings and not share them with others." But the time had come for her to "come out," she said, for the sake of others who might be more vulnerable than she, and for the sake of the church that it might more faithfully exhibit the mind of Christ. Before her "coming out," she had written (with Letha Scanzoni) a book titled *Is the Homosexual My Neighbor?* in which she had argued passionately for the church's openness to gay and lesbian persons. But in that book she had not revealed her own sexual orientation.

So it was at a meeting of the Presbyterian General Assembly, albeit in an independent advocacy group, that I came face to face with the issue of human sexuality and Christian faith, not as an academic or a political matter, but as a reality now embodied for me in a human being whom I knew beyond any shadow of doubt to be a Christian, and my sister in Christ.

That, of course, did not resolve the issue for me. But it did focus it mightily in my mind and heart. And it drove me with renewed urgency to the scripture and its interpretation, and to a reexamination of the witness of the church through its doctrine, its polity, and its praxis in relation both to its own members and to those outside the camp. Whatever one may conclude from such a journey as that, this much is clear to me now: the first step in any faithful reconsideration of the church's traditional teaching and practice in this matter must be to cease talking *about* homosexuality in the abstract, and to begin talking *with* its own baptized sons and daughters as beloved children of God and as pilgrims together in our common journey of faith seeking understanding.

In this quest, scripture is crucial for Reformed Christians. But what does scripture lead us to believe and to teach concerning homosexuality? Faithful interpretation of scripture cannot be for us a simple quoting of texts ("the Bible says . . . "), as most would agree. Rather, it is a matter of discerning what the texts mean in their contexts and in ours, and always testing scripture against scripture.

What we now know is that there are six, and only six, Bible texts that appear to refer either directly or indirectly to homosexual matters. There is some disagreement among biblical scholars concerning what those six passages refer to: whether pederasty, temple prostitution, promiscuity, or same-sex union. But even if one were to grant for the sake of argument that all six refer to homosexuality as it is understood today, are they to be interpreted as a command of the Lord, or as the counsel of leaders in light of their time and circumstance? On this also, biblical scholars are not agreed. Evidence of this disagreement is well documented in two recent books published in 1996 by our own Westminster John Knox Press. *Biblical Ethics and Homosexuality: Listening to Scripture,* edited by Robert L. Brawley, presents the papers from a consultation of twenty-four Bible scholars, mainly from Presbyterian seminaries, gathered at McCormick Theological Seminary in August 1995 to consider biblical ethics and homosexuality. *Homosexuality and Christian Community,* edited by Choon-Leong Seow, presents essays written by fourteen members of the faculty of Princeton Theological Seminary, gathered around three topics: what the scriptures say concerning homosexuality, how we are to interpret what scripture says on this matter, and how we are to live faithfully in light of what the scriptures teach on this subject. Both books reveal that there is no consensus on these matters among our church's biblical and theological scholars today, but rather a wide diversity of understanding of these things.

How then are we to proceed? Does the scholarly diversity leave us without guidance? And do we find comfort in that diversity, or is it a cause for alarm? For me, the diversity just now is reassuring, for it demonstrates that the whole church is on a pilgrimage together as we seek to live faithfully in these troubled times. We cannot legislate consensus; rather, we are called to listen together as carefully as we can, both in the seminaries and in the pews, for the leading of the Holy Spirit that we might know and do God's will in matters such as these. In such a time, it is surely right to be quite skeptical of any who would speak arrogantly or immodestly about what the Bible says about homosexuality. What we can do, and I believe should do, is speak humbly and charitably with one another, bearing witness to the light as we see it, to the extent that God gives us light, always being eager to be taught and corrected by the light that God gives to others. For true it is that even if we should have prophetic powers, and understand all mysteries and all knowledge . . . but have not love, we would have gained nothing.

Speaking as modestly as I can, and with as much love as God gives me toward those who may see things quite differently than I, let me bear witness to the light as God gives me to see it, in view of the account of my pilgrimage as I have recounted it in these pages.

First: The fact that Jesus, so far as we know, never once spoke about homosexuality is far more persuasive to me than the fact that some few others did. Jesus had much to say about anger, greed, lying, ambition, divorce, and lack of compassion. But about the manner in which faithful and committed partners should or should not make love, Jesus seems to have had nothing to say. Whatever the six passages elsewhere in scripture may mean—those that appear to speak to what we today refer to as homosexuality—I cannot assuredly say. But the silence of Jesus about same-sex relations makes me far from sure about that matter's priority in the mind of the One who sent him.

Second: The central criteria of people's acceptance in the church, according to my understanding, are (a) their confession of Jesus Christ as Lord, and (b) the evidence of reality of that confession—that is to say, the fruit of the Spirit in their lives. The latter may at times require us to reconsider traditional assessments of who is acceptable in the church and who is not. Simon Peter found it so when, in response to his proclamation of Christ to the Gentile Cornelius, evidence of the Holy Spirit's blessing became visible and indeed audible in the life of this outsider. Under the circumstances, Peter broke new ground as he became obedient to the heavenly vision: "What God has cleansed, you must not call unclean." I know personally too many wonderfully gifted Christian women and men whose lives are shared with partners of the same sex for me any longer to regard them as unrepentant sinners. It pains me deeply that these Spirit-filled women and men are so regarded by significant portions of the church today.

Third: We are told by some that same-sex orientation is a conscious choice, and that this choice is contrary to the will of God. It is important that we be aware of the link between those two assertions. If one judges (for whatever reason) that same-sex orientation is evil, then one *must* regard it as a conscious choice lest God be found to be the author of sin. Scientific inquiry becomes unnecessary. I do not wish to regard this view unfairly or uncharitably; I simply say that I find it utterly unconvincing. It addresses the issue abstractly as though homosexuality were simply a matter of logic. It is my observation, however, that sexual attraction is neither abstract nor logical. It arises out of the deep recesses of one's personal identity. What I find to be persuasive is the personal testimony of scores of homosexual women and men whom I have come to know and respect, each and every one of whom have told me that they did not make a conscious choice for same-sex orientation, that they were born such, and that it is as much a part of their created nature as the color of their eyes. Those who argue otherwise make no such argument from their own experience, yet seem ready to make judgments concerning the experience of others. Medical science is thus far inconclusive in the matter. Until more light is given, I will trust the testimony of those who personally experience homosexual attraction—often at cruel social, economic, and ecclesiastical cost—rather than rely on the speculative judgments of those who have never experienced such same-sex attraction.

Fourth: In the current debate concerning the ordination of persons of same-sex orientation, I am more and more often hearing opponents of such ordinations protest that "the real issue is not homosexuality but biblical authority instead." I find myself less and less persuaded by that protestation, even though those who say it doubtless believe what they are saying to be true. All of us, however, are liable to self-deception when we attempt to speak of our own motives in debate. Slowly and reluctantly, I have come to the conclusion that the most elemental issue in this debate is not biblical authority, but is how one feels at an emotional level about homosexuality itself. I can appreciate feelings of revulsion that one may experience in thinking about any form of intimate sexual practice different from that which one regards as "normal" or socially acceptable. Such feelings make it difficult to assess one's real motives in moving to condemn what others are moved to affirm. In the past, scripture has been passionately called to witness by the church in defense of human slavery, in opposition to the ordination of women, in defense of war, in support of capitalism, and in support of state socialism. If the majority heterosexuals and the minority homosexuals can talk with one another long enough and openly enough that the majority can get beyond its feelings of disgust concerning things unfamiliar, we may in time be able to search the scriptures together with open hearts and minds. We might then be enabled to hear together what the Spirit has to say to the churches.

→ Lillian McCulloch Taylor is an ordained Presbyterian minister. She has recently served as associate director of continuing education at Princeton Theological Seminary, and as interim co-pastor of a local church. She is also a Certified Christian Educator, has served as a Presbytery Christian Educator, and as director of the library at Columbia Theological Seminary. She is married to the Rev. David W. A. Taylor, who was until recently general secretary of the Consultation on Church Union. They have two children: the Rev. Frances Taylor Gench, who is Professor of Biblical Studies at Gettysburg Theological Seminary, and Dr. David Taylor, Jr., who is a geophysicist in Greensboro, North Carolina. And they have two grandchildren. Now retired, Lillian and her husband make their home where she was born, in Elizabethtown, North Carolina. She continues to serve as book review editor for *The Presbyterian Outlook*.

12

Yes, Use My Name

➤ MITZI G.HENDERSON

The request had taken me by surprise. "I guess I can serve, only please don't use my name," I had said. As soon as the phone call was over, my mind began to race. It was the fall of 1984. We were recent arrivals in the community, new to our church, new to our presbytery. Now I had been asked to serve on a presbytery task force on homosexuality. How had the caller discovered that one of our children was gay? This was a secret we had guarded for five years, never revealing it to our former congregation or our colleagues in presbytery and synod work there. Who else knew? Who would be on the task force and how would I explain my presence there?

When I was growing up in a Presbyterian church in Illinois, knowing the names of the other children and adults in my church made me feel at home there. Being called by my name by my Sunday school teacher, the minister, the members of that congregation made the message of God's love for me real because they knew and cared for me. Now, as a grown-up, I found I wanted to hide my name, to be anonymous.

The dozen or so people who gathered for that first task force meeting were all strangers to me. In some way that was comforting. They knew much more about the presbytery than I did, I thought. So I could keep my counsel, sit back and let them take the leadership. But as we introduced ourselves we learned we all had at least one thing in common. Every one of us had agreed to serve only on condition that our names not be used.

As we revealed more about ourselves, we discovered we were all supportive of gay and lesbian persons in the church, and felt that study and discussion were urgently needed. But we weren't sure we were ready to bear the costs of taking the lead. Most of us were deeply involved in the life of our congregations. Lay and clergy alike, we feared being ostracized or forced out of our congregations. We worried about personal rejection, attacks upon our reputations, our families, and our commitment to the Christian faith. And that fear was keeping us closeted.

The first hurdle we faced was finding someone to stand up and speak

YES, USE MY NAME ⇐   81

for the task force at the next Presbytery meeting. No one was willing. With deep misgivings, I finally agreed to be the one.

I had never been a spokesperson, even for the causes I had supported. During the civil rights movement, the feminist movement, and the anti-war movement, there had been leaders, inside and outside the church, who I felt were better informed and more capable than I. And they had stepped forward to inform and inspire my generation. That was their call. I was sure my call was to be a mother, Sunday school teacher, and church and community volunteer.

But this time, I sensed, was different. Unlike those times, I could see there weren't people stepping forward to speak out about this cause, especially inside the church. I was aware of the appalling ignorance about gay people and their families. This time I knew more, from personal experience and from research and reading, than my friends. I knew more than the elders and clergy I worked with. I knew more than the many religious leaders who claimed expertise on homosexuality. I not only knew more, I felt deeply angry and frustrated by the ignorance, the silence, and the unwillingness of large segments of the church to engage in open, respectful discussion of our deeply differing understandings. I hoped the task force could begin that discussion. So I had said yes.

I spent many sleepless nights in the weeks before the Presbytery meeting. I wondered how to communicate how isolated and fearful we felt, the hateful things we had heard, and how important it was to begin to learn more about the people affected by the rancorous debate about the role of homosexual persons in the church.

The day arrived. Standing before the meeting, and with pounding heart and dry mouth, I described what it had been like studying the General Assembly reports on homosexuality in the spring of 1978, then the following Christmas learning one of our four children is gay. I talked about our shock, our struggle to understand, our wrestling with the Bible, and our fruitless search for pastoral help. I spoke of the need for the church to minister to its own, its sons and daughters and their families. I spoke of the need for information for pastors and lay people. I spoke of the Christian commitment of our son and other gay Presbyterians. Finally, I spoke of the work the task force hoped to do.

Often I have seen God's action in my life only in retrospect. I was totally unprepared for the enormous liberation I felt in finally telling the truth about our family—and the opportunity the presbytery had to begin a new openness to our gay and lesbian members and their families. But I was even more unprepared for the call that came that day in presbytery.

Like the "still small voice," it came after the anxiety and turmoil of the speech. It came in whispered confidences, in anguished phone calls, in the response of my own congregation whose delegates were at the meeting. I had realized that others needed help. But it was a shock to have them turn to me for pastoral care.

My husband, Tom, and I had been attending a small, local chapter of Parents and Friends of Lesbians and Gays (PFLAG), a family support group. In the preceding several months we had come to know well other families and several gay and lesbian persons. We had begun to realize our gay son was not the problem. He was just fine, and so were we. It was our fear of others' reactions that had kept us silent and fearful, even in the church. We had become tired of the stigma that was unfairly laid on us all. That experience had been a powerful motivation for agreeing to the presbytery talk.

When the task force next met, one of the goals we set was to find a way to supply pastoral assistance to families and to gay and lesbian persons. Clearly, the churches of the presbytery were not doing that, and few showed any interest in developing such a ministry. So another mother from the task force and I took on the task of establishing a PFLAG group for families in the San Jose area.

We had heard Janie Spahr was assisting the formation of a PFLAG chapter in Marin County, and we sought her counsel. Then we began phoning, located a few other local families, secured a grant, found a Congregational church to meet in, and set the date. We hoped for a dozen people, and over fifty showed up that first evening. It was a revelation. People spoke from the heart, in wonderment that there was a place where they could be honest and be received with love and understanding. Many were active members of congregations. Few had dared to approach their pastors or priests.

Meanwhile, the task force tried its best, securing books and offering workshops. But the presbytery had little interest. Eventually we disbanded. In contrast, the Parents and Friends chapter flourished. Little by little I realized this was the ministry to which I was called. It is a pastoral ministry that the church finds itself unwilling or unable to do. Torn by differing understandings, dogmas, deeply seated convictions, and an aversion to disagreement, the church preferred to argue in the abstract. Meanwhile, families and their gay and lesbian loved ones were finding in PFLAG the care they were not receiving from the congregations. And I was devoting increasing time to the help line, to newsletters, to speaking.

As so often happens, one step leads to another. I took a nonvoting position as secretary of the national board of PFLAG. Then a volunteer job as regional director. Finally, in 1992, I was elected the national president. For four years I was a national family spokesperson of the renamed Parents, Families, and Friends of Lesbians and Gays. This was not what I set out to do. I agreed to speak to the presbytery, not to Congress and the media. But when you answer a call, you can't be sure where it will lead.

I would never have embarked on this work had I realized what lay ahead. There were so many skills I didn't have, so many things I didn't know, so many challenges to face. "You are going to hell, and taking society with you," the radio caller told me. "Last night I tried to kill myself, and I am afraid to go home tonight" the young gay teenager confided to me. "Your testimony must be no more than five minutes," said the congressional aide. And learning to fax, e-mail, conference call, set agendas, handle personnel conflicts, raise money—all the organizational things I had never done before—was daunting. But each new challenge has been a call to grow, to learn. Fear of failure has been kept at bay by the awareness that the world is in God's hands.

Along the way my life has been enriched by a myriad of wonderful, committed persons: political activists and closeted families, children of gays and transsexual persons, Presbyterian families in crisis, and families liberated and "out." These persons have been a gift. Their courage, their faith, has shone in their lives.

I have also been exposed to the downside of this work. I have met and worked with people who have been harassed, assaulted, and murdered. An unreasoning fear and hatred of homosexual persons, so often reinforced by religious rhetoric, is routinely dismissed in the discussions I hear in church. Yet it is the reality we live with, and it must not be ignored. As in other periods of social ferment and change, the Christian church, in its many manifestations, has been riven with arguments over what position to take—leadership or opposition.

It has been eighteen years since we learned our son was gay. Eighteen years of debate, dissension, despair, and development in the life of the Presbyterian Church. It has been painful and inspiring for us to be Presbyterians, as silent members, as spokespersons, as colleagues and adversaries in the ongoing struggles to bridge the chasm between gay and straight people in the church.

The needs are great. First, the need for a safe space for gay, lesbian, transsexual and bisexual persons and their families. This cannot be assumed today, certainly not in the church. Second, the need for an understanding of sexuality. Third, honest discussion about the Bible, its authority, its interpretation—not just about sexuality, but about all facets of life for the Christian. Fourth, an exploration of how the Bible and experience validate or invalidate each other. And fifth, the call to be the community in which we mediate Christ to one another. All of these transcend the homosexuality debate but are intertwined with it.

It isn't easy work. The temptation is to give in to our fatigue and walk away from this hassle. Yet, seeing the Spirit at work in the lives of so many people, gay and straight, keeps our faith renewed. We are not about to abandon the church, though the church might wish we would. So we struggle on in hope. And we delight in our companions on the way.

I know now God called me that day in presbytery—to a work I never anticipated. To talk about being "called" is to invoke the uneasy reactions we Presbyterians have to such terms as "born again" or being "saved." It isn't that we don't experience those realities. But that language carries such a freight of cultural and religious baggage that we hesitate to use the words for fear of sounding too self-righteous or smug. But the truth is that we do experience God calling us to lives we would not necessarily choose for ourselves. I have always believed the church is God's agent in the world and in our lives. Though they could not know it, and I did not immediately understand it, the church indeed was God's agent in 1984, calling me to this new and most rewarding ministry.

✦ Mitzi Henderson is an elder and lifelong Presbyterian. She and her husband, Tom, married for forty-two years, have two sons, two daughters, and seven grandchildren. She has held positions with the League of Women Voters and the American Cancer Society. Mitzi has served as trustee of McCormick Theological Seminary (1983–1992), and as chair of the More Light Churches Network (1989–1990). She is a member of PFLAG (Parents, Families, and Friends of Lesbians and Gays) and was national president of this organization from 1992 to 1996.

13

And So It Was

⤞ LYDIA HERNANDEZ

I had just arrived at the airport in Dallas and was taking the shuttle bus to my hotel when a young man with red hair addressed me, saying, "You must be Lydia Hernandez. I am Chris Glaser and I will be sharing the workshop with you on justice." I was impressed by his friendly enthusiasm. At that time I was the director of the Office for Racial Justice and Reconciliation for the Presbyterian Church (U.S.A.) based in Atlanta, and during the '80s I was often invited to speak on racial justice issues. The event in Dallas was sponsored by the Synod of the Sun and I was looking forward to being in Texas, since I was born there.

After our workshop, during which time Chris gave his testimony as a gay person and advocated the rights of gays, I was chastised by a woman of color who demanded to know why I had shared the platform with a homosexual person. I remember being taken aback by the criticism and defended myself by saying that anyone who is treated unjustly should be defended, no matter who the person might be. As a woman of color I remember the following words from my mother and quoted them to her: "*Mal es mal y bien es bien.*" In other words, wrong is wrong and right is right, whether you are brown, black, white, purple, or upside down.

Meeting Chris and being challenged about my own behavior was the beginning of my awareness of the discrimination suffered by gay persons like Chris within the church. Of course, I had other experiences that brought the subject to my attention, but I was awakened to the reality of yet another group of people who felt that they suffered injustice, and I could not ignore their pleas for a hearing.

Certainly I had had previous contact with gays and lesbians in the church, but the subject had always been hushed. Maybe I should say that "the word" was always out on who was supposedly homosexual and "the word" always carried a note of caution. I distinctly remember a time when I had gone to Atlanta for a committee meeting and had been invited by some staff members and others to go to a party. The party turned out to be all female; the male staff person who drove me to the party said, "Be careful, one of the women may make a pass at you." My response—facetious—was, "So what?" I felt that this male staff person was feeling insecure about seeing all of us women together, since we crossed racial lines and generational lines.

During the late '80s I was at Bossey, the Ecumenical Institute in Geneva, to study spirituality for a year and had been appointed as a volunteer in mission to work with the director and associate director. I spent many hours in the library reading religious poetry and biographies of spiritual leaders, and in general studying Christian spirituality. I discovered that many of the authors of religious poetry had been persons who were persecuted and had suffered on behalf of just causes. I read books about women's spirituality—this was fun because the authors included women of color. It was during this time that I decided to read *Uncommon Calling*, by Chris Glaser, not only because I knew Chris and wanted to read what he had written but because I wanted to become more informed. Little did I know that God was preparing me for a new task.

The students who came to study at Bossey came from all over the world, which made the theological discussions especially interesting. The students were challenged not only theologically but also spiritually. Many of them confided in me, and some of the more painful stories were by gay men and lesbians. As this was an international community, I experienced firsthand the international dimension of the pain suffered by these very committed Christians. Of course many causes were equally painful—indigenous people of Hawaii and Australia had their own struggles; there were those suffering under the apartheid system of South Africa; and women told horror stories about sexual exploitation in Thailand and the Philippines. Again, it was confirmed that injustice and suffering have no national boundaries. Studying and practicing the Reformed spiritual disciplines of daily prayer, scripture reading, and journal writing freed me to become involved with those who through their lives of Christian witness were transforming their communities. This experience, through the power of the Holy Spirit, transformed me so that I too could become a transforming agent. Being transformed is intrinsic to the spiritually disciplined life, that one may love God and God's world. (Love God and your neighbor as yourself: Luke 10:27.)

And so it was that reading the book by Chris opened up the possibility for me to become an agent of love for those in pain, gays and lesbians. As if God knew that I myself needed concrete support, I got a call from Chris saying that he and his partner were in Europe, and could they come for a visit. Of course I was elated, but then Chris asked if he could speak publicly. The answer from the director was no. However, the volunteers who served at the supper tables heard about this, and by word of mouth news got out about Chris's visit. Therefore, after supper many stayed to hear Chris testify and were enlightened. I was mildly reprimanded but felt it was a small price to pay for what we had all received in return.

After I had started seminary at Johnson C. Smith Seminary in Atlanta and had done a year-long internship at Bossey, my aging mother's illness brought me back to Texas, where I continued my theological studies at Austin Seminary. It was now in the early '90s, and my nephew Mark approached me and announced that he was gay and was about to become actively involved at his university in support of gay rights. He asked if he had my support and would I share this with the family to see how they would feel? Within our culture, family is important and many believe that whatever the family members do, their actions will reflect on the family. Obviously, the goal is not only to maintain family unity but also to preserve *la dignidad y honor* (the dignity and honor) of the family. Our conversation took place during Christmas and all the family was gathered, so I went to talk with the teenagers about this. I had no more than said, " I need to talk with you about Mark," when one of them said, "What? That he is gay?" My son quickly interrupted and said, "Mom, we all know about Mark, it's the adult part of the family that you have to talk to." With that, they dismissed me, and I sat down at the kitchen table to talk with my eighty-three-year-old mother. I said to her, "Mom, I want to talk with you about Mark and the fact that he is gay." She asked, "What is the problem?" I told her that he planned to become an activist in the gay movement and was likely to make the news on TV and radio. I went on to say that this might upset some adult members of the family. Her response was, "Let it be their problem. We have all known about Mark for many years and have loved him; why should that change now?" She then said, "How about another cup of coffee?" End of conversation. And Mark became an activist and, yes, made news in the papers and on television.

Mark, like a proper Chicano grandson, continued to make visits to his grandmother and he shared his activities with me during these visits. It was during one of our many conversations that he challenged me to study the whole homosexual issue. He felt that as an advocate for social justice I should become actively involved in support of gay and lesbian rights. He also challenged me directly as someone studying theology, because he is convinced that the position of the church is the basis for much of the homophobia and anti-gay and anti-lesbian legislation found in much of our society. In a course on ministry with women, I along with four other female students decided to study homosexuality/lesbians. I learned much in that semester. Also, Mark had introduced me to some Chicana lesbians, mainly his friends; they were my teachers on the subject. I participated in the first commemoration of those who had died of AIDS within the Chicano community in Austin. The event, sponsored by Informed Sida (an AIDS organization), was held not only to remember those who had died but also to educate the Latino community.

During this time I was also working on a theological anthology by women of color, which I used as an opportunity to interview or at least get to know Chicana writers, musicians, and artists, some of whom were lesbians. What lingers in my mind about the interviews and in simply meeting these Chicana lesbians was their spirituality. Some spoke of the rejection they had experienced within the church, but they were able to separate what they saw as a weakness in the church from their belief in God. Again, I believe that God was preparing me for yet another task, where my faith would be tested, because it was precisely in the middle of taking the course on ministry with women that a young seminarian asked me and a male student if we would be interested in celebrating the commissioning of the Rev. Janie Spahr, a well-known lesbian in the Presbyterian Church (U.S.A.), during a worship service in the chapel.

I said I would be interested in sitting down to discuss the matter. As the oldest person in the group, and the only one with an organizing background, I said that my commitment was firm but that I also needed everyone else's commitment to see the whole event through. I warned the students from the beginning that it was my assessment that the event we were about to ask the seminary to sponsor would be controversial and that if we didn't make a solid commitment to make it happen, not only would the worship service not happen but our small group would be destroyed. And so began a very interesting chapter in my life and the lives of others. I had survived other controversies so I was not surprised when the student council changed its mind, first yes, then no, or when the faculty was in favor but then got nervous and began changing the rules and some just backed away from their original support when we didn't follow the changing rules.

The Evening Prayer Service was held under the sponsorship of an ad hoc committee of students. The Rev. Janie Spahr came to visit the campus. I was accused of politicizing the pulpit, of trying to divide the church, of leading the young students astray, but what I remember the most was the students making biblical and theological arguments pro and against the ordination of homosexual persons late into the night as we worked on the liturgy for the worship service, as one them said, "All for the glory of God." Yes, at the end, despite the pain, tears, hard work, and accusations, I felt that we had all experienced the grace and mercy of our Lord Jesus Christ—by reaching out in love to those whom the church is trying to shut out.

During Janie's visit someone hosted an evening with her so that people might have an opportunity to meet her informally. It was late and most of the crowd had left except for those of us in the support core group, and I remember Janie asking, "Who made all of this happen?" One of the students said, "I did!" I smiled inwardly and said nothing. The best gift a good organizer receives is to be able to walk away from what one has organized without being recognized. And so this has been my experience working within the Presbyterian Church for all of these years of ministry, being called to different tasks and roles by God and just walking away when the task has been completed.

Little did I know that the Lord was preparing me for an even larger task. I had been asked as a seminarian to serve as the resource person for the General Assembly committee (1993) dealing with the issue of ordination of homosexual persons. At first I was scared to undertake such an awesome responsibility, but in the end I agreed to serve in this capacity. As one who has always believed that the church of Jesus Christ is big enough to take in the glorious diversity that exists in the universe, I was prepared to listen to all who wanted to testify in good faith. I suppose the most moving moment for me at the Orlando General Assembly was the testimony by hundreds of gays and lesbians and relatives on the platform. I was sitting with another Mexican American clergywoman who with tears in her eyes asked, "How can you want ordination in a church who will be excluding most of these faithful committed Christians?" I suppose I was holding on to a greater vision, the biblical image of the remnant as spoken by Jeremiah: They will come "from the north . . . from the farthest parts of the earth, the blind and the lame, those with child and those in labor"—those who had been shut out by the society in Jeremiah's time (31:8). And I guess I believed that the church would someday embrace the same biblical image despite the continued racial discrimination against people of color by some people within the church. But I suppose the reason I didn't give up on the church is not because of the strength and weaknesses of the institutional church but because God in Jesus Christ is in charge of all of our lives. The Presbyterian way is to study, study, study, and maybe someday act. And so it was that the General Assembly voted to study the issue for three years. Many of us, however, had come closer to understanding some of our homosexual brothers and sisters, and through their powerful witness, with the help of the Spirit, had been graced.

Later, as a missionary to Guatemala ordained by the Greater Atlanta Presbytery, I could give thanks to God for the privilege of being able to serve and give witness to the love received through Jesus Christ. As a professor in the Presbyterian Seminary in Guatemala, I was honored by inquisitive and enthusiastic students. Many were curious about the rumors they had heard about my church, the Presbyterian Church (U.S.A.). "Not only does your church ordain women as pastors and elders, but now your church may be ordaining homosexuals!" they exclaimed. Then they asked, "What do you think about the subject?" My response was, "I know how I think, but what do you think? You will soon be leaders of your church and as pastors will be dealing with these very basic family issues." Needless to say, the discussions were animated and *caliente* (hot!) but always in a Christian spirit. Some of the students came to me in private and confided that homosexuals were already in leadership positions within the church and some confided that they had relatives who were gay or lesbian, so they were pleased to be able to discuss the topic openly. And so it was that even in Guatemala, God's love and mercy abounded.

The vote on the ordination of homosexual persons had just been taken in Albuquerque at the 1996 General Assembly, when as a committee assistant, I looked toward the back of the auditorium and saw a large group of people gathered to march in support of gays and lesbians. I looked again, and my nephew Mark was one of the people standing right in front. At that moment I was lifted to my feet and took the hand of another assistant, a young woman who was crying, and I said, "Let's go join the procession, my nephew is right in front." As I walked to join the line, many others began to take my hand and join the procession. I was sad that more people did not join in, that there was even a need for a procession to stand up for the rights of those who are different. Yet I was elated and gave thanks to God that we could be a part of "the remnant" in the biblical vision that Jeremiah described: They will come "from the north . . . from the farthest parts of the earth . . . the blind and lame, those with child . . ."

Now I see my role as an enabler, as one who can help others stand up and speak out. I ask God to give me the strength to sweep away any hesitancy or reluctance that I may have about loudly proclaiming what we as Christians believe—that we are all God's children. Through God I have been transformed, but it is a transformation still in the making. It is not yet complete, nor is it easy. Just writing this article has been a struggle. A good friend, familiar with church politics, advised me not to become publicly involved in the debate. "You have already had enough crucifixions in your life," she said. She is well aware of how ordained ministers and activist clergy are often handcuffed from doing their work or from being recommended for other jobs when they take stands on so-called controversial issues. But I had no choice; the Lord took away any excuse I made for doing this.

Too often, when we are called upon to put our faith in action, we back down, we shy away, we are scared about what others will think. I ask God for the ability to look at a person *from within*, not focus on the exterior; to be more accepting and understanding, not judgmental. And I thank God for people like Chris Glaser, Janie Spahr, my nephew Mark, and so many others, who have taught me about the fullness of human life. From their example, and by the grace of God, I have gained the strength to join in the procession. It is a procession that not only supports gay/lesbian ordination but also marches in support of all persons and groups who are treated unjustly.

✦ Lydia Hernandez, an ordained clergywoman, recently served three years as a missionary in Guatemala. She is the former director of the Office of Racial Justice and Reconciliation for the Presbyterian Church (U.S.A.) and was based in Atlanta.

➤14◄

Going on a Journey

✦ JACQUELINE BROVOLD

> *And Jesus responded to the Pharisee lawyer and said: "'You shall love the Lord your God with all your heart, and with all your soul, and with all your mind.' This is the great and first commandment. And a second is like it: 'You shall love your neighbor as yourself.' On these two commandments depend all the law and the prophets."*
> —Matthew 22:37–40

As a child I was taught by my family and by my church that we human beings are just that: *we* human beings. No *us* versus *them*. And all of us, *all* of us, are made in God's image.

As a child I was taught that God makes no mistakes. There is in each of us something valuable, something of God. From my childhood neighbor and friend Jerry, slowly dying from muscular dystrophy, I learned that beauty and gentleness and humor sometimes come in a body confined to a wheelchair with a voice as soft as a whisper. From another childhood friend, David, I learned that being developmentally disabled has nothing to do with the zest and vigor of one's faith and sense of joy in being alive.

Early on it occurred to me that the diversity of the human household is a diversity reflecting God's own innate diversity: the Trinity. And if God is somehow Community, we, too, are meant to be community.

When I was young, nobody I knew talked much about homosexuals. Not at home. Not at church. Just at school, sometimes. But by high school, I had gotten a clearer vision of homosexuals from my culture: *they* were odd, strange, maybe even crazy. *They* had made choices, ugly choices, which made *them* bad people.

They were dangerous and we were to avoid *them*, though I wondered sometimes how we were to avoid *them* since *they* were also nameless and faceless.

Somehow in our culture, homosexuals were not included in the human family, though we seemed quite at ease affirming the humanity of murderers, despots, and rapists. How strange this was . . . how confusing.

It was blood that began my journey out of this confusion.

It was blood that shoved me toward Love.

I was eighteen, freshman year of college, and down the hall from me lived two roommates we will call Leah and Rachel. Leah was the gregarious one, always joking, always singing. Rachel was quiet, more serious. Leah was from a big city; Rachel from a farm near a small town. They were immediately, awkwardly incompatible. By the third month of school, they were not speaking. And soon a literal line had been drawn through the room, each young woman staying in her own territory. I knew that the cold silence resulted from many conflicts, not the least of which was Rachel's suspicion that Leah was a lesbian.

One wintery night, I walked out of my dorm room and saw drops of blood leading down the hall. I followed them to the door of Rachel and Leah's bedroom. Rachel was in bed reading. Leah was not there. I asked it I could walk over to Leah's side of the room and Rachel nodded. And there I found a pool of blood. I called for Rachel to come look, but Rachel kept reading.

When I contacted one of the counselors, I learned that others had found Leah after her attempted suicide and had gotten her help. She was in the hospital. She would be all right.

A few of us mopped up Leah's blood. And as we did so, I wondered if I had in some way contributed to this night, this girl's pain. Had I, too, pulled away from her, afraid of her? As we cleaned up Leah's blood, Rachel sat on her bed and read. "I don't want to see it. I don't care!" she said. And my eyes were opened to the reality of another side of oppression—not open hostility, just this cold, grim, self-righteous hardheartedness masked as something morally superior.

That night I found Rachel's response much more frightening than the possibility of Leah being a lesbian. And that night, incited perhaps more by the injustice than by compassion, I began a new journey.

As the years passed, I discovered that homosexual people were not so nameless and faceless after all. They were there among my neighbors, my friends, my colleagues in teaching, as well as in the media and marching in the streets. No longer did homosexuality seem strange, deviant, or bad. It is only another way of being fully human. And there is a great diversity among those who are homosexual, I discovered—just as there is among those of us who are heterosexual.

Yet most of the people I knew who were gay or lesbian were also very closeted. This was a secret about them, not a mere fact. And I accepted that.

But then I went to divinity school, finally answering an old and still recurring call that God apparently had put on automatic redial. It was in divinity school that I encountered lesbian and gay students, teachers, and administrators who were not hiding, not in closets, but out and loose and sometimes very loud.

Their pain, their outrage, and their struggle for justice within the church called me to be more than a closeted friend. As I watched intelligent, talented, and faithful friends—who also happened to be homosexual or bisexual—prepare for ordination, I saw their options. They could lie to their presbyteries, conferences, or other governing bodies, hide their sexual orientation and "pass," or they could come out and be denied ordination.

I remember sitting with Diane and Peter and so many others as they wondered why God was calling them into a church that did not love them or honor them or want them.

And I wondered, too. For I believed that their sense of call was strong and right and good. And I believed that the church needed them. And it was then that I knew it is not enough to care from a distance or hold a friend as she weeps over dying dreams. It is not enough to be silent as the church follows fear instead of Love.

Love demands action. Love demands solidarity. Even to the end and through the end.

AIDS has touched each church I have served, almost always in the form of a young homosexual man. And I have watched families and whole communities become transformed because of their love for this person, for that person. Love changes how we see, how we receive, how we give, and how we feel. Somebody we love is not part of *them;* he is part of *us,* she is *ours.* And Love cracks those hard walls of self-righteousness, breaks down barriers of fear, knocks holes in armor long polished. Love is more powerful than hate.

I have seen it again and again.

In the last church I served, the session had already declared the church to be an inclusive community a year before I arrived. But that was not enough. It was too passive an act of justice. Too quiet a response to the pain. And it was our gay and lesbian members and others who supported them who asked the church through the session to consider being part of the More Light Churches Network.

It took us a year as a church to talk, to listen, to confront, to pray. It took us a year of hard work. A year of telling and retelling our stories.

Through this process, I reminded the session that we would only become part of the More Light Network if we truly felt called by God to do so. This was not only a social justice issue; it was also a theological issue.

When the session did act by consensus to become a More Light church, we knew that in affirming our sisters and brothers who are gay, lesbian, bisexual, or transgendered, we were not only standing up for them, but with them, beside them. Indeed, we were no longer trapped in the old "us" and "them" model. It was a new day. A new model. A new form. One circle filled with men, women, youth, and children. Loving one another. Loving ourselves. And most of all, first of all, loving God.

⤝ Jacqueline Brovold is part of a rainbow family of Nigerian, Chinese, English, Scottish, and Norwegian heritage, which includes her two children, Abraham Robert and Nellie Ming Li. She has been an ordained minister of Word and Sacrament since 1984. She received a bachelor of arts degree from St. Olaf College, a master of arts from Washington University, and a master of divinity from Harvard Divinity School. She lives in Miami, Florida, where she is pastor of Pinecrest Presbyterian Church.

15

I Live in Hope

✦ ELLEN BABINSKY

I remember our conversation so well, though it was years ago. Diana Vezmar-Bailey and I had already been friends for years that day we had lunch together. The day in Minneapolis was sunny and pleasant, and we were outside. As our conversation meandered over a variety of topics, I sensed that there was something in particular she wanted to talk about. Diana being Diana, I also knew she would get to it when it was appropriate for her to do so. And she did. She chose her words carefully as she helped me to understand her self-awareness as bisexual. Somehow I wasn't surprised, although I will say that until she began to talk about herself, I could not have guessed. After she told me about herself, she began to talk about our friendship. She said something to the effect that she had never thought of me nor responded to me in a sexual manner. My response is a clear memory: "Well, why not?" We broke into gales of laughter, laughing and laughing in delight and joy, knowing that our friendship would continue, and being so grateful in the knowing. As the years have passed since that patio conversation, there have been many difficult times, and Diana has always invited me to stand with her.

Diana was not the first gay person I had known, for I had met several gay folk during my seminary years. But Diana and I were in a special relation, for we had shared our deepest soul struggles in seminary and in the years following. Diana was and is written on my heart. And so she led me, guided me, talked with me in the years that followed that conversation over lunch. I remember so well the days surrounding the time she spoke at the presbytery meeting when she set aside the practice of ministry in the Presbyterian Church (U.S.A.), a time she describes in the book *Called Out*. I was in graduate school at the time (at her encouragement, I might add) and was not able to be with her in this difficult time. I wept bitter tears, not so much because I feared for Diana but because I feared for the church. It was that speech, and Diana's leaving the denomination, that pushed me into the fray. I chose then, and choose now, to work unceasingly for full inclusion in the leadership of the Presbyterian Church (U.S.A.)

Since coming to Austin, Texas, where I teach the history of Christianity at Austin Seminary, I have come to know students who are wonderfully talented Christian men and women, who either have been denied or will be denied leadership because of their life partners. In these committed people the church has lost excellent leadership for the future. One former student, Jay Kleine (whose story also appears in *Called Out*), removed himself from the call process before any congregation had an opportunity to receive his gifts for ministry and leadership. He came to my office to tell me that he was going to remove himself from the process because he could not and would not lie to his committee of care about his orientation and soul-partner; to do so would violate the ordination vows for which he had been preparing himself. I wept bitterly at his words. As far as I know, he has been dropped from the care system without the presbytery having had an opportunity to hear from him. He would have been such a fine minister of Word and Sacrament. From his chapter in *Called Out*, one can see that he still proclaims the gospel.

Babs Geminden, another former student, has removed herself from the process because the stress of the lie was becoming too much. She wrote a letter to the members of her care committee, but apparently the letter was never read in committee and never read before the presbytery, so the church may or may not be aware of the loss of her leadership. She remains so incredibly pastoral and has such integrity as she goes about her work as a licensed chemical-dependency counselor. Troubled persons are touched by her healing presence; the troubled church is not. From time to time, I weep bitterly for the church's loss of Babs's ministry.

I am thankful that the courageous witness of gay and lesbian Christians offers the church some opportunities to be aware of this loss of future leadership. Michael Rodriguez, again a former student, had developed an extremely effective ministry in a children's home. His reputation among the persons in leadership in his presbytery was excellent. His ability to communicate the grace and truth of the gospel to the children in his care was stunning, and they loved him. He came to the painful decision to leave the practice of ministry because he knew deep down that people loved who they thought he was; they did not love a gay man. Toward the end of his time at the home, he gathered the staff, speaking separately with four of the boys, and told them about himself. He asked one thing of them: that they remember that they had known a gay man and that he had never hurt anyone. Then he went before the presbytery and publicly declared that as a gay man, he could not continue in deceit when the gospel impelled him to tell the truth. He is still an active member of presbytery. As he told me these things on a commencement Sunday afternoon later in the year, I wept again.

I lift up these vignettes because, although I weep bitter tears, I also live in hope. I live in hope, first and foremost, because I live in the power of the resurrected Christ, in whom all things are made new, who beckons us onward, and who never separates from us or leaves us alone. In Christ is our peace, our purity, and our unity. Second, I live in hope because by grace I have been given the gift of wonderful friendships and support from lesbian and gay people, and I am thus surrounded by life-giving hope that comes through the grace and power of the Holy Spirit. And third, I live in hope because of the story of Christianity. The difficult times we are facing now are no more difficult than were faced by any of our forebears in the Reformation era of the sixteenth century. I could no more recant my convictions than could the Reformers in their time.

What we all need is a safe place that can become a laboratory for fidelity—fidelity in the deepest sense of soul sharing and caring. In my heart of hearts, what I yearn for is that the church be that laboratory for deep fidelity, to one another, to one another's partners, to our children, to one another's children. In the name of fidelity, of soul caring and sharing, why should not those who survive us after death inherit? In the name of soul caring and sharing, why should not those whom we love receive the benefits of health care? For the past twenty years, by the grace of God, I have been given the gift of a life partner. Because he is male and I am female, the state and the church recognize us as married and confer upon us all kinds of privileges. Last spring he underwent very serious surgery, and it was only right that my health care plan cover it, for he and I have made a life covenant to care for each other, to bind our souls. I want to honor, and I do so honor, and I declare that we must honor such life commitments to partners made by all persons, regardless of the gender of the life partner.

Most important, however, is Christ, who has called us and names us as Christ's own, in life and in death. To exclude from leadership any of those whom Christ has called is to silence the One whom we proclaim to be our center and our hope. To exclude these persons from leadership is to render Christ voiceless in our midst. Trusting in the empowering presence of the Holy Spirit, I desire to work "to hear the voices of people long silenced" (*Book of Confessions* 10.4.70). I see the issues surrounding the full inclusion of gay, lesbian, bisexual, and transgendered persons as human and theological concerns of the heart that still have not been explored deeply enough. I want us to extend full inclusion to them, not because we know what we are doing and no further dialogue is necessary; I want full inclusion because we do not know. Let us in humility claim that we do not understand everything about what we declare, and let us continue to be in dialogue, with all voices empowered to speak the truth in love. May the power of the Holy Spirit continually engraft us into Christ.

⬧ Ellen L. Babinsky, Ph.D., is Associate Professor of Church History at Austin Presbyterian Theological Seminary, Austin, Texas, where she has served on the faculty since 1988. Following in the footsteps of both her grandfathers and her father, who were pastors in the Reformed Church in America, she was ordained in 1976 to the ministry of Word and Sacrament in the Presbyterian Church (U.S.A.). She has a bachelor's degree in philosophy from Earlham College in Richmond, Indiana, a master of divinity degree from McCormick Theological Seminary in Chicago, and a master of theology degree from Luther Seminary in St. Paul, Minnesota. From 1976 to 1983, she was associate pastor at Westminster Presbyterian Church in Minneapolis. She earned a doctorate in the history of Christianity from the University of Chicago in 1991. Ellen is married to W. Douglas Sampson, an ordained Presbyterian pastor and interim specialist. They are the parents and stepparents of six adult daughters.

16

The Presbyterian Church
Is Not a Safe Place

✧ CYNTHIA CROWNER

When I was a teenager in 1968, the youth group activities at First Presbyterian Church in my hometown just didn't grab me. I felt called to much more than a weekly meeting with six or seven peers for conversation and Cokes.

But our Presbytery Youth Committee had more creative and compelling programs that kept me in the church. During the summer of my sophomore year, the presbytery offered a one-week workshop for youth with dramatist Don Marsh, to teach us how to use improvisational drama in our home churches. Each day, we read scripture together and then through poetry, contemporary music, mime, and improvisation, we made those scriptures come alive for our times. The program woke us up to the power and meaning of our tradition because it connected with the issues we were facing: the Vietnam war, sexual liberation, civil rights, and the profound questioning of culture that was the hallmark of the '60s.

Ours was an exceptional group of teens—some had tremendous musical skill, others a passion for literature, and still others a flair for the dramatic. But all of us were creative and fun loving and wanted to make the connection between our faith and the demands of our times.

That week together generated an amazing experiment in authentic Christian community. In fact, I have never experienced such a profound sense of church as I did during that workshop and the two years that followed. Out of the workshop, we formed "The God Squad" (forgive the name!), a traveling drama group sponsored by the presbytery. We went from church to church in our region, presenting our style of worship. Always scripturally based, our services featured the disturbing poetry of the "beat" poets, the folk and rock music of our generation, and our own original improvisations, which aimed to make the biblical stories relevant to our times.

To some in the pews, we were a scandal. But to the younger set, we were like a collective Pied Piper, our numbers growing each time we met at a new church in the presbytery to plan our next worship service "happening."

After a summer of our itinerant ministry, the presbytery had the good sense to know they were onto something and decided to continue to sponsor our troupe one Sunday a month in churches of our area. After all, where else in the nation were young people flocking into Presbyterian churches in 1968? The troupe continued for several years in this way, the personnel changing as the original members graduated and went off to various colleges while new younger people signed on. But the spirit of Christian community continued—a community marked by a depth of reflection, creativity, celebration, mutual support, and sharing of our resources and our love. It may have been the best thing the Presbytery Youth Committee had ever launched.

In 1986, eighteen years later, I went back to my presbytery, this time as a candidate for ordination in the Presbyterian Church (U.S.A.). I made a date to get together with one former God Squad member who was still living in the area. It was a grand evening of reminiscing and catching up. As we were about to say goodnight, my friend said hesitantly, "Cindy, I have AIDS. I don't know how to tell my mother and I don't know where I can go for support." The news of his illness knocked the wind out of my sails. But almost as devastating was my friend's admission that he did not know where to turn for support. How could it be that after such a profound experience of Christian community less than two decades earlier, this man had no confidence that the church would be there for him? He was probably right. Our little band had been unique and was unorthodox. We would have supported him without question. But from his perspective, the institutional church was not to be trusted. Since 1978, the church had gone on record that gay and lesbian Christians were second-class members. How could he trust such an institution with his pain and confusion?

At that moment, I committed myself to being a part of his support team, even though I lived thousands of miles away. But I was able to put him and his mother in touch with one or two of the people in that presbytery who had been involved with or supportive of our "God Squad" experiment. We knew they could be trusted. These Presbyterians were just about the only people who were able or willing to support that family through the two excruciating years that ensued. My friend was the first in that town to be diagnosed with AIDS. It was horrifying to receive phone calls from him and his mother as they told stories of rejection: the local funeral homes had refused to make arrangements to deal with his body after his death, fearing contamination. He was told they would not allow even a memorial service in their chapels because of the nature of his disease, his "sin." Initially, the caretaker at the local cemetery told the family that my friend's body could not be buried there, but he later relented after we got on the phone and complained. It was a nightmare of rejection when he had to be hospitalized as well. My consciousness was raised to new heights about the devastating power of homophobia. At the same time, I was relieved that at least some Presbyterian individuals were there for this family whose need was so great and whose disillusionment with the church was so profound.

I have known for many years now that this man was not the only person in our "God Squad" who is gay. Yet it never occurred to me that anything would disqualify them from full service in our church. They had already proven their commitment to the way of Christ.

So it has been painful and disconcerting to be an ordained Presbyterian minister these last eight years as we have struggled with the issue of gay ordination. I have learned the scriptural, ethical, theological, and political arguments as to why qualified gays and lesbians should be ordained as elders, deacons, and ministers of the Word and Sacrament. I have organized programs in local churches and at presbytery meetings in an attempt to educate sister and brother Presbyterians. I have preached on the issue. I have been at the key presbytery meetings to strategize, speak out, and cast my vote.

But I know in my heart that anyone opposed to ordaining gay and lesbian people is unlikely to change his or her mind through argument. I am convinced that it is deep, loving relationships that open us to the movement of the Spirit and free us to change. It is when we come to know a gay or lesbian Christian "up close and personal," the way I did in our "God Squad" experiment, that those barriers become irrelevant. When you know and work and worship with someone whose calling is compelling and whose gifts are great, sexual orientation is just not an issue.

So how does one come to know a gay or lesbian Christian? It is a dilemma—until we make our churches "safe places" where gay and lesbian people can be at home, they will continue to pray next to us in the pew, sing next to us in the choir, direct our choirs, organize our Christian education programs and mission projects, and even preach to us from the pulpit without our knowing they are homosexual. Or they will leave the church when the burden of keeping their secret becomes too much to bear. Either way, this is tragic.

From 1988 until 1994, I served a congregation that became a More Light church. The openly gay man who worked with the session for a two-year period as they studied the implications of taking this step did not give up or lose heart. But some time after we had finally voted to declare ourselves "More Light," he did leave the church without explanation. I suspect that his story is like many others I have heard from former Presbyterians. Instead of the church being a source of spiritual sustenance and empowerment, it had become an arena of struggle, a drain on his spirit, a burdening yoke. This caring individual left our church family, a family intent on becoming inclusive. But I think he needed a congregation where he could give that yoke over to Jesus so he could be freed to serve as God was calling him, where he would not need to be a single-issue Presbyterian. Even in our "safe space" church, he was still defined by his sexual orientation; he still wasn't thoroughly understood, and he would probably have been called upon to organize the congregation to defend itself from the denomination.

Today I serve as the director of the Kirkridge Retreat and Study Center, an ecumenical and independent center in Pennsylvania with a strong and proud twenty-year history of gay and lesbian Christian programming. In my two years here, I have met many dedicated, prayerful gay and lesbian Christians whose worship, music, and theological reflection are among the most powerful I have ever experienced. The mutual support and pastoral care this community offers its members is unparalleled. Kirkridge has become a spiritual home for Roman Catholics, Evangelicals, and Protestants of all varieties, including gay and lesbian Presbyterians and their families, whose local churches are no longer welcoming or understanding. Some of these folk continue to struggle within their congregations and denominations. But each year, more and more people seem to be leaving in search of authentic Christian community, one that accepts them fully for who they are, affirms their leadership abilities, and responds to their willingness to serve.

It is a privilege to be a part of this ministry, to provide this mountain retreat "home" for these outcasts. I am convinced that Jesus would have embraced them. He was, after all, the teller of the parable of the Good Samaritan. Jesus would have embraced gay and lesbian Christians precisely because they are ostracized by a church that is more concerned with purity than with compassion, more defensive about law than open to grace. As a church, we walk on tiptoe on the opposite side of the road and leave the wounded person bleeding and unattended.

Demographers say that up to 10 percent of the U.S. population is homosexual. Is it possible that 10 percent of our denomination's members are gay or lesbian? Will we lose 10 percent of our membership as a result of changing our Constitution? Perhaps most of that 10 percent have already left us. I believe even more is at stake. Over the past two years, I have become aware that our church's crisis affects even more than gay and lesbian Christians and their families. I speak regularly to heterosexual clergy in our church who are feeling emotionally and ethically torn. We feel the deep need to be authentic, to stand up publicly for our convictions that gay and lesbian Christians be recognized as children of God with the same rights and responsibilities as heterosexual members. If our Constitution is changed to deny this basic equality, must we leave the church? Or will we stay and put up with a "separate but equal" kind of arrangement in order to maintain our ordination vows, even when we feel it is fundamentally contrary to the gospel of Jesus Christ? Do we follow the law of the church or the higher law of our consciences? Is the unity of the church or the comfort of our positions worth the sacrifice in our self-respect?

I have written this essay carefully to avoid "outing" anyone, gay or straight. I am aware that each Presbyterian has to make choices for him- or herself. Yet there is part of me that wishes we could all muster the courage to say who we are and what we believe. But then, I am in a privileged situation. I am heterosexual, already ordained, and serving an ecumenical and independent agency. I am not in a position where I can ordain anyone, so presumably I am not a threat to the church. I have some freedom to speak and act. Not all Presbyterians are so free.

Four or five years ago I had the opportunity to see another old friend from our original "God Squad" at a national church gathering. I had not seen her in many years. We had shared this deep experience of Christian community and I was eager to reconnect. We found a quiet place away from the hubbub and sat down for a few minutes to catch up. But when I asked her about her personal life, she replied, "Cindy, please don't ask. The Presbyterian Church is not a safe place."

✦ Cynthia Crowner has been a Presbyterian minister since 1988. She graduated from San Francisco Theological Seminary and served as Associate Pastor in Global Peacemaking at the Montclair Presbyterian Church in Oakland, California, for six years. Since 1994 she has served as the Director of the ecumenical Kirkridge Retreat and Study Center in Bangor, Pennsylvania. Since her days on the campus ministry staff at Cornell University in the 1970s, Cynthia has been active in promoting greater justice in U.S.–Latin American relations.

17

Facing Fears:
"Cast Outs" Calling Us toward Healing

➤ ELIZABETH HINSON-HASTY

Walking into the Southern Baptist Convention was quite an experience for me as a twelve-year-old girl. Hundreds of people rushing into the convention center created a scene filled with chaos and drama. In a frenzied atmosphere women, men, and children hurried to reach the door. We were destined to witness the election of a new president and vote on a variety of issues relating to church business. As my friend and I approached the door, a middle-aged woman and her young son, carefully clutching a stack of brightly colored papers, greeted us. The little boy thrust toward me a fist gripping one of the pamphlets and asked me to take it. I accepted his offering and began plunging once again into the crowd hoping this time to reach the entrance. Only glancing at the pamphlet after receiving it, I bore it as if it were a banner signifying my own importance upon entering the large meeting room.

Sitting on one side of the main floor, we had a good view of the crowd. Letting my eyes wander around the room I looked over the "messengers" to the convention, those entering, those campaigning, and those visiting. Perplexed by the atmosphere of confusion dominating the conference, I began reading the pamphlet. The title read, "Every Third Child Dies from Choice." A small, colorful picture accompanied these opening words. Looking closely at the picture I distinguished a bloody mass positioned atop a caption reading, "Aborted Baby." Thumbing through the pages of the booklet, I saw more pictures of aborted fetuses, each picture uglier and more bloody. Horrified by this brochure, I feared what the convention might offer next.

Anxiously, I watched as the meeting began. After spokespersons brought forth issues for debate, time was allotted for discussion. "Messengers" from the crowd descended upon a number of microphones placed throughout the room. From there they voiced their opinions on the issues presented. One woman passionately expressed her discomfort with the ideology that was being showcased. Two men ushered the woman out of the auditorium. My stomach sank. The redness of my cheeks warmed my face as I

looked down at the floor. I was afraid that if I voiced my views, I would
be the next one to be quieted.

These memories of my experience at the convention do not fully describe my feelings of alienation, but they illustrate how people are silenced
by others in the name of God. For many years I stayed away from the
"church." I feared that someone might try to force me to believe what they
believed or act in a manner they labeled appropriate and faithful. I have
since affirmed my belief that there are many ways to be named faithful.

Presbyterians welcomed me four years ago with outstretched arms.
Our church gave me a seminary education. I continue to enjoy an open
environment where I can study, grow, contribute, give, and receive.
Through my study and experiences the seeds of openness have grown
within me. A desire to welcome others has been nurtured. As a Presbyterian by choice I have learned that possibilities abound for us to be open
and intentional about seeking inclusiveness.

Considering the perspective of my own acceptance into the Presbyterian church, I find it very hard to understand or embrace the guideline
proposed by the 1996 General Assembly of the Presbyterian Church
(U.S.A.). The guideline encourages the presbyteries to allow the ordination of gay, lesbian, bisexual, and transgendered people only if "they"
abstain from sexual activity. I can feel the body of the Presbyterian
church who greeted me with open arms crossing them in refusal of others yearning for *full* acceptance.

As a married, white, heterosexual woman I do not share exactly the
same struggles as people discriminated against because of their sexuality.
I do know, however, what it feels like to be afraid to celebrate fully who I
am. I have been afraid to celebrate my own gifts and talents because of being unsure whether or not others would accept me. I have also been afraid
of being rejected by my faith community because of my ideas and gender.
I believe that memories shape our experiences. Memories serve either to
enable or hinder us. Recognizing my own fears enables me to stand in solidarity with others who are afraid of being denied the right to celebrate
themselves as full participants in our faith community.

Fear tactics that are used to persuade people to behave or to believe in
a certain way have a lasting impact. Gory brochures and abusive methods
of control instill fear. Removing people from the mainstream reinforces
our fears, anxieties, and apprehensions. Choosing to separate gay, lesbian, bisexual, and transgendered people makes us afraid. Fear stifles our
consciences and limits our actions. How have we been conditioned to fear
these individuals?

Numerous studies have been conducted regarding the legitimacy of those claiming to be attracted to persons of the same gender. "Nature or nurture?" we have asked. Celebrating sexuality within the church is continually questioned and often problematic. Poking and prodding into so-called different lifestyles has occurred as part of routine investigations. What statistics, stereotypes, labels, and studies cannot offer us is direct involvement in the lives of those experiencing oppression.

Consider the story of one person I believe to be excluded by our church, a woman who I will call "Marta."[1] Envisioning her face, taking a moment to visit her life, provides an opportunity to experience the feelings of someone cast out from our church.

A vibrant and energetic young woman, Marta volunteers to help with weekly church events. She is an elder and has served as clerk of session. She works hard to encourage the success of the ministries of her particular church. Singing in the choir, serving as a lay liturgist, and regularly attending worship services—all are part of Marta's weekly discipline. Committed to her call, Marta helps others in her greater community. She brings a rich contribution to our church. Colorful experiences, thoughtful reflection, faithful gifts of time, talents, and financial resources all are given to us by Marta, who continues to enrich her church.

I met Marta at a dialogue focusing on issues concerning faith and gender. At a roundtable discussion, ten women shared stories about their particular churches. Our conversation was peppered with joy and pain. Marta turned to me and said, "I have never felt like I can be truly honest about who I am in my church. I am not sure if people could handle it. I am afraid to go to church with my partner." Gluing my eyes to the floor, I did not really respond to what she said. I did not fully understand.

At the close of our conversation our attention was drawn to the front of the auditorium. A woman called all gay, lesbian, bisexual, and transgendered people to come to the center of the room. Surrounded by the crowd, the people in the center gripped each others' hands and raised their arms with great excitement. Marta had joined the circle.

When she returned to the table, one by one we hugged her. Marta breathed a sigh of relief and said, "I have never been able to truly be myself at a religious gathering before. I have never even been able to show a picture of my family." In a moment of triumph someone cast out of her church felt the unconditional affirmation of a faith community.

As I reflected on my encounter with Marta, I felt angry and powerless. Why could she not have been assured that the arms of the faith community would be open to her if she revealed her entire self? Why could she not share family stories and pictures with her congregation? What message is she receiving about God through the treatment and actions of her church?

Convincing the members of our church that discrimination is wrong may be an easier task than getting them to think about ordination of homosexual persons. Ordination has long been revered as a "special" call God issues to leaders of the faith community, a call extended to those professing belief in Christ who promise to be part of God's work in the world. For many years, ordained people were thought to be somehow "other than" the rest of the congregation: more learned, more holy, perfect examples of moral behavior, and, perhaps, even more committed. Homosexual, bisexual, and transgendered people have not been thought of as worthy of being uplifted to this status of perfection. In recent years, I think we have all discovered that we are cut from the same fabric. Ordained people are imperfect. We all miss the mark.

Ordination is not a "special" call because ordained people are better than other members of the greater church. It is a special call because of the promise evident in their God-given gifts for proclamation and because of the belief that these gifts should be used for the betterment of the church as a whole. When contemplating the story of Marta's involvement and promise for ministry, how can anyone say she is not worthy to be an ordained elder or minister? Her commitment is already present. The gifts have already been given. The call has already been made. In light of her talents, obvious commitment, and openness, could God afford not to call her? Can we afford to exclude her or hundreds of other people in her position?

Could we be prompting Marta and others to believe that they cannot fully disclose themselves before God, as part of their particular church, or to reveal themselves to the faith community as a whole? Do we continue to cast people out of our community because they miss some indistinguishable mark that makes them worthy of acceptance? When considering Marta's story, I think that we are guilty of practicing discrimination, exclusion, and rejection. I believe that it is now our responsibility to share the hospitality God offers to us, unconditionally, with all those called to be full participants in our church.

Encountering the pain of Marta's fear that she would not be accepted by her faith community is one reason that I choose to stand in solidarity with gay, lesbian, bisexual, and transgendered people. Seeing the faces of other people whose lives have become intertwined with my own fuels a fire empowering me to become partners with others aching for change. I have not taken this stance without a great deal of thought about all people whom it affects. Personal reflection, conversations with friends and mentors, involvement in student activist groups, theological study, and biblical understanding all undergird my decision to join in the struggle to move toward freedom from oppression in the church.

In closing, I would like to offer the image of another woman who also remains unnamed. This woman is not someone whom I have met personally, but she is nonetheless an inspiration for me to stand with the other. In Matthew 15:21–28 is recorded the story of a Canaanite woman who comes to Jesus for healing.

At first the story seems relatively simple. The woman comes to Jesus for help. Initially, he and the disciples refuse her. Jesus and the woman talk for a bit, and he compares people of nations other than Israel to dogs. Distraught, she confronts him, reminding him that even dogs receive the crumbs from their master's table. He listens to her plea and pronounces her faith to be great. "Let it be done as you desire." He is pleased. She is pleased. The woman exits the scene.

A surprisingly different picture of Jesus is drawn here from the one we might expect. Jesus, who appears tired of the crowds and the business of healing, wants to ignore the woman. Speaking metaphorically, Jesus compares the Israelites, the children, to the Gentiles, the dogs. His words represent the thought that the salvation offered by God would first be extended to the Israelites and then, as the word spreads, to people of other nations. Jesus seems to wonder how far the ministry can reach. Would it be fair for a Canaanite woman to receive the same healing offered to the Israelites?

The "pesky" woman refuses to accept Jesus' retort, "It is not fair to take the children's bread and give it to the dogs." Defying all societal boundaries, she comes to Jesus as a Gentile, someone ritually unclean, a single, poor woman with a daughter, totally isolated from any family support. She risks talking to him and engaging him in a verbal sparring match. The proper thing for her to have done would have been to accept his answer, to leave with it willingly. But this Gentile woman does not leave. She says, "Yes, Lord, yet even the dogs eat the crumbs that fall from their master's table." Out of desperation to save her daughter and belief in Jesus' power to transform, she begs him to extend the grace offered for Israel even to the "dogs," to those outside the chosen circle. She risks talking about a daughter in need of healing because her daughter's life is valuable to her. Her life is precious enough to demand healing and the transformational power of Christ.

The Gentile woman bears a double witness in this story. First, there is power in the woman's witness as a Gentile, one not associated with Jewish tradition, to Jesus as a miracle worker. And, second, her faith, one without doctrinal identity or endorsement by the growing faith community, is a faith that acts upon consistent trust and willingness to risk everything. Its effect enables Jesus to see the situation in a different way.[2] Something is revealed to Jesus by his pausing to hear her story. A new perspective appears to free Jesus to respond, to heal, to become again the channel by which God's redeeming presence is known to the woman and her daughter.

In this story the author of Matthew focuses upon Jesus' humanness. He desired to refuse the woman, to ignore her. Jesus knew what it was like to have the feelings we have, to be tired of confronting people, to be tired of trying to get it all done, to know how hard it is to challenge others to seek openness. What sets him apart as the Christ of God is that he becomes the healer anyway. The challenge to extend the community to *all* in need of healing is taken. The community opens itself up because of the Canaanite woman's struggle, after encountering her story and understanding the pain that she felt. In Jesus' actions, we recognize our own responsibility as a faith community to be open to Christ's power to transform unjust practices.

I believe that this story says something of great importance in relation to the struggle for justice for gay, lesbian, bisexual, and transgendered people. From the pages of scripture a Canaanite woman reminds us that we can have an effect on the work of God in the world. Jesus' eventual acceptance of the Canaanite woman represents for us that understanding and feeling the pain of others can solicit openness and provide an initiative for change. We see Jesus as the healer Christ, the possibility for transformation. Where will we be challenged to extend healing to the Canaanites in our own faith community? What witnesses are calling us to be transformed on account of the testimonies of their struggles?

Choosing to stand in solidarity with gay, lesbian, bisexual, and transgendered people means that we allow our own experiences to become intertwined with the "other." It means that we continue to challenge ourselves to tell the stories of those living under the weight of oppression. In the coming year what will the stories of these witnesses mean to all the people of our community?

I believe that allowing ourselves and encouraging others to see the faces of individuals, of Marta, call us toward healing. We have the opportunity to be part of healing. Policies that instill fear, inflict pain, and deny all of us the right to celebrate the diversity of gifts offered to us can be changed. We can seize the possibility to transform exclusionary practices in our church.

Marta's story puts the call toward healing into perspective. Can we, as members of the Presbyterian Church (U.S.A.), handle fully accepting God's lesbian, gay, bisexual, and transgendered people? I believe so. We can handle surrounding Marta and others by a circle of affirmation and healing, fully, unconditionally welcoming *all* people into our faith community.

Resources

The New Interpreter's Bible, Volume 8: *The Gospel of Matthew*. Nashville: Abingdon Press, 1995.

Russell, Letty M., ed. *Feminist Interpretation of the Bible*. Philadelphia: Westminster Press, 1985.

❖ Elizabeth Hinson-Hasty is working on a Ph.D. degree in the Department of Theology and History at Union Theological Seminary in Virginia. A candidate in the Louisville Presbytery, she hopes to be ordained to teach in a seminary or university upon graduation from Union. Currently, she lives in Lynchburg, Virginia, with her husband, Lee.

18

An End to Silence

→ MICHAEL E. LIVINGSTON

This is hard to do, so accustomed to public silence am I in this matter. I have long believed that sexual orientation is a given, a gift from God, and been a friend to those in my circle who know themselves to be gay, lesbian, or bisexual. In personal conversation or informal small-group settings I do not hesitate to say what I believe about this last frontier. In my preaching I have been an advocate for the radical inclusion and the abundant grace that confronts me in the story of Israel and the gospel of Jesus. God's love embraces the breadth of humanity, the community of nations, all of creation. I have been identified, and believe myself to be regarded by others, as one who supports the ordination of—to use that curious phrase—"self-avowed, practicing," homosexual persons.

Still there is a part of me that knows I have held back, been too restrained, too careful in the public debate that has so divided us these days. My motives have been honorable, if no longer adequate for me; to keep the conversation going, to be viewed by all as trustworthy, to avoid the inevitable conflicts that separate and divide us into hostile camps. So let's tell the truth. Personal conversations and support aside, I have not spoken with the kind of specificity and clarity I believe to be required today, privately and publicly, so that we may fully embrace gay men and lesbian women who are not just among us; they are us.

I want to speak my heart, not argue biblical interpretation or genetic engineering, critical as those are to these discussions. Surely my convictions find patronage in scripture and science, and these and other disciplines inform my living. Given the repository of tradition and heritage, of intellect and thought, with which we can never dispense, there is yet a dimension to experience which is wholly subject to the present moment and to a future ripe with the possibility of new creation. It is that personal daily engagement of life—what I say, think, and do as I encounter others and come to be and know myself—that I want to explore.

Memory is often self-serving. I used to think with some frequency and say occasionally that my language as a preacher has almost always been inclusive. I assumed the best of myself, conferred intuitive good sense upon my homiletic practice. Well, I checked old sermons from my first years in ministry and found enough "Fathers" and "men" to hold a Promise Keepers meeting in Yankee stadium. Our memories are more romantic than our marriages. That leads me to question what I might want to offer as truth—a childhood and adolescence free of name-calling, stereotyping, participation or silent acquiescence in schoolyard taunting: "Hey faggot, queer, dyke."

My own experience of vulnerability to a loving but sometimes violent father predisposed me toward defense rather than persecution of those attacked. Yet I cannot say that I did not accept passively, if not share, the homophobia so deeply entrenched in our society and culture. Thankful that I cannot remember ever actively and knowingly engaging in abusive behavior toward a gay or lesbian person, I am certain I hurled at others the despised designation "sissy" and swaggered to avoid it myself. Now it is an epithet I consider both sexist and homophobic.

As a child I didn't know what a homosexual person was, but I knew what it meant to be called a sissy. For a boy to be so named meant you were thought to be like a girl, a queer, a fag. You couldn't be called much worse. I don't know anyone who welcomed and embraced the term, though I can recall a few who, with a kind of indignant and wounded, yet defiant, pride, claimed for themselves a reality most of us knew nothing about. In our ignorance we battered, silenced, and marginalized people in our families and our neighborhoods we could just as easily have loved.

As I grew older, it became clear that homosexuals, men especially, were not uncommon and in my African American community, including the church, they were at least tolerated and their gifts and abilities celebrated. While it may have seemed curious to me and my friends that most gay men were musically and artistically inclined, a "goes with the territory" manner of thinking, we would never have suspected that many other gay men, hidden from view, engaged in what we would have considered the normal range of pursuits.

And while our community did indeed appreciate the gifts of visible gay men, there was a tacit understanding at work similar to the insidious "don't ask, don't tell" formula we have elevated to the status of law today. As I read it, the contract went something like this: "We will tolerate you in our midst, even celebrate your gifts; for your part, be silent and keep your relationships out of sight." The attitude, in adult society, bordered on "We know, so what?"

I do not mean to sanitize the infectious bile hurled at homosexual persons, the derision that might be released at the slightest provocation—anger or the opportunity for a good laugh at the expense of another. Ultimately, I must defer to those gay men and lesbian women in the African American community whose experience may have been harsh and embittering well beyond the romanticism of memory.

Suffering invisibly were those men whose demeanor gave no hint of homosexual orientation and lesbian women who were for the most part, at least in my experience, deeply closeted. Lesbianism was simply much less an issue, and this is easily understood in the context of the patriarchy of the larger society and of the black community as well. What two women might do together just didn't seem to matter as much. Memory of my early years is remarkably devoid of encounters with lesbian women until I was a teenager.

One summer, late in high school, I was involved in a project with kids from other churches around the city. I had long, stimulating conversations about civil rights and race (this was around 1966) and other matters in intense relationships in that vigorous and life-changing time. In conversation with two girls one afternoon, they told me they were lesbians. I was stunned, never having experienced such openness on this subject. I remember quite well the feeling that dominated my emotions: rejection. I felt they were rejecting me personally, and recall trying to be likeable and attractive to them! The matter of race is terribly important to me, and yet I have to work to remember that the girls were white. Their race was much less significant to me in those moments than was their sexual orientation. I don't mean to suggest any ranking of conditions; such an exercise is demeaning and fruitless. For me on that afternoon, lesbian sexual orientation wore a particular face, two faces, and a deep subconscious internal conversation continued evolving toward today.

I don't remember the day I met Joseph, dead now of AIDS. I'll never forget him. He was a year or two behind me in college. He was loud and large—six feet three inches tall and weighing nearly 300 pounds. He was aggressive, brilliant, and impetuous. With him I felt as though I was in one of those bumper cars at the amusement park. Cars racing and crashing madly here and there, stopping and starting, random and chaotic. His mind was quick and agile, restless. He told stories that made life into a continuous soap opera. Every encounter was fraught with hidden meaning, pregnant with mystery. If someone known to us passed by, Joseph knew something hidden and unexpected about them; some pivotal turning point in an intriguing subplot just developing. If someone unknown passed by, Joseph invented an identity, a story line; he quoted dialogue that resolved dramatic tension or raised the stakes to breathtaking and suspenseful heights.

What I would have thought incredulous, if left alone to ponder, seemed reasonable, inevitable in his telling. His visits were most often wild rides. I held on, not too tight, and tried to keep my balance. When necessary, I tapped on the brakes or pointed out large boulders dead ahead. Now and then, in the midst of fantastic flight he would touch the ground and show me where he lived, why he flew so high. He almost welcomed what he considered my bourgeois, antiquated (meaning too religious), pre-seminary perspective. He listened. It seemed to do him good. I'm glad for that now. When he left after a visit, tired or bored, reality resumed a familiar shape.

Joseph was gay and public about it. They don't make closets that big. He was as beautiful a human being as any I have ever known—not because of his sexual orientation, or in spite of it. He did what he could with what he had been given by God and humanity. He painted on a large canvas in bright colors. The images are still vivid, memorable.

He was exhilarating and exasperating. He made me laugh, think hard, learn patience and tolerance. I marveled at his energy, his great will and wit. His suffering saddened me, so much of it unnecessary, I believe. It led him toward his death. There is no one to blame, and I do not apologize for him; it would not serve him well. His grandiosity and bravado were a response to a set of norms he just didn't fit. A gay black man with talent and brains. There have been others. Think about it: Where are the most well known? They are dead or gone to Europe. The rest are in the closet.

I remain awed by his love for me, for its spontaneous ignition and its unswerving constancy.

Joe found me before he died. Called me to let me know, warn me, prepare me; to be angry, to look back, reassess, resolve. I didn't invite him into my life. He just came in. I am immeasurably richer for his too-brief company.

"Michael, honey, that's enough." Lying in his hospital bed a few days before he died, David told me he wanted no more of the water I was trying to get him to drink. He was also tired of his battle against AIDS and prepared to die in the providence of God and on his own terms. David died in the company of his longtime companion. In the last months of his life, at home and in hospitals, he wished to be alone with his companion. He made it known that he would prefer not to receive visitors apart from me and Carol Belles, the secretary in Miller Chapel at Princeton Theological Seminary where David worked as music director and I was pastor and director of the chapel.

This heightened tension in an already anxious environment led to considerable confusion, sadness, and frustration in the seminary community.

David did not want to become a poster boy for AIDS, and in the months before he could no longer work he resisted any suggestion that he was seriously ill. Was he in denial? Was he afraid to speak up for fear of persecution?

David lived by the traditional unwritten rules. He was discreet about his sexual orientation. He did not make an issue of it. He did not participate in the gay rights movement, much less advocate for gay rights or the ordination of gays and lesbians within the church. He played no public role in the discussions at the seminary on these matters. He pretended to be less than his whole self. He divided his life into separate spheres in nonnegotiable orbits. I believe that such restraint exacts a profound toll upon those who exercise it. He paid that toll in order to be able to offer his extraordinary gifts to the seminary and to the church at large.

Those rules were broken for David when the Princeton Declaration (written to "[uphold] the PC(USA) in the decision not to ordain individuals engaged in homosexual practice") was widely circulated by its authors and those who supported its content. While, quite clearly, the declaration was not directed at anyone specifically, I believe David took its meaning personally. He regarded it, in a subtle and profound sense, as a declaration against him, and from members of the very community to which his vocational life was devoted. His work was not just a job in some capital-generating enterprise; it was the ministry of one who grounded his being in the body of Christ. He was deeply wounded and angered by this episode.

My counsel to those in our community regarding David's desire for privacy was for respect for the terms he set for his own death. While I might offer the same counsel today, my perspective has changed. These were not his terms; this isolation, the silence and invisibility, this straight arm against intimacy. Those are the old rules inverted. Do you see the disquieting symmetry that defines the incongruity and inanity of this moment in, of all places, the church? Dying, David insisted we continue to adhere to the rules. Gay man dying of AIDS? What gay man?

I do not suggest or suspect, on David's part, cold calculation here. At his greatest moment of vulnerability, when he needed the energy flowing through every available synapse, he simply reverted to the demeaning familiar charade. In a sense, David died in a deafening silence, all but invisible to those for whom he lived. In this there is an alternately chilling and wondrous irony: in death he was celebrated for precisely the person he was—a marvelously gifted gay man of deep faith.

It was my great joy to work with him in the worship life of the seminary. It was my honor to serve him as he lay dying.

I have studied the scriptures and engaged in informed theological discussion in the company of the good minds and good hearts in our seminary and in the church at large. I know and have known, love and have been loved by, gay men and lesbian women whose character and gifts, whose sense of call by God to ministries of every kind, is surely as deep and abiding as my own. I trust that God may work through anyone God chooses: at the table of remembrance and in the fields of mission far and near, to bring to bear upon a destructive and unloving world, the love, grace, and justice of the gospel. Surely not enough of us are engaged, with any urgency, in this work. Majorities have been wrong before, for centuries. You will understand how an African American person in this church and society would come to that conclusion.

I look forward to the day when we are all out of the closet, men and women of homosexual orientation and the friends and family members who affirm them. With courage and determination let us put an end to the silence and the invisibility. In love, let us seek the healing warmth of God's grace in the wounded body of Christ.

⋆ Michael E. Livingston is the campus pastor and director of the Chapel at Princeton Theological Seminary. A 1971 graduate of the University of California at Los Angeles, he was awarded the master of divinity degree at Princeton Seminary in 1974 and the master of theology degree in 1991. Prior to his present position he served as director of admissions at Princeton Seminary, pastor of Hollis Presbyterian Church in New York City, and assistant pastor of St. Paul's Presbyterian Church in Los Angeles. He is chair of the Committee on Ministry of the Presbytery of New Brunswick, and editor of *Liberation and Unity*, a Lenten devotional guide published by the Consultation on Church Union. He is married to Nancy Rucker Livingston and they have two children, Aaron and Megan.

19

The Gift of New Eyes

✈ JOHN J. CAREY

In February of 1985 I went with a group of Presbyterians from the Presbytery of Florida and the Presbytery of Mobile on a study trip to Central America. The purpose of the trip was to enable us to see the realities of politics, power, and poverty there. Confident that such firsthand exposure would give us all new insights into the problems of Central America, the planners of this trip organized it around the theme "The Gift of New Eyes."

When I was invited to contribute to this volume, that topic came to mind as an appropriate way to describe my intellectual and personal pilgrimage into a changed awareness of gay and lesbian persons. That pilgrimage took me longer than it should have, in part because my journey has been a gradual process of making connections between a whole range of justice issues.

My coming to a "gift of new eyes" makes more sense if I clarify whence I started. I grew up in Fort Wayne, Indiana, in the 1930s and '40s in a working-class family. My family was a strong church family, but in those days sexuality was not discussed much in our home, let alone in church educational materials or from the pulpit. Gender roles in middle-class America were clearly defined in those decades, and the mysteries of sexuality were discussed privately by girls and boys in their intimate peer groups. There were no sex education classes in the schools. The first lessons of sexuality were learned slowly and generally awkwardly through teenage dating. Places of special interest and intrigue for teenagers were backseats of cars, drive-in movies, hayrides, and beaches with blankets. I never knew that there was such a thing as same-sex attraction until I was a junior in high school, and then the awareness came through some jokes about male "queers." All through high school and college I did not know any boys or girls who had obvious same-sex preferences. I virtually never thought about gay or lesbian persons, but my latent sense was that there were very few such persons; that such persons were certainly abnormal; and that they lived in a mysterious and silent subculture. Such people did not infringe on my world, however, and their problems were certainly not my problems.

After college, seminary, marriage, and graduate training, I began my professional career at Catawba College in Salisbury, North Carolina, in 1957, and moved to Florida State University in 1960. That move coincided with the emergence of the civil rights movement in the south, and Tallahassee, being the home of Florida A & M University (the state's historic institution for blacks) was in the middle of that turmoil. As university chaplain and subsequently as vice-president for student affairs at Florida State, I was heavily involved on racial fronts (1960–65) and with the emerging student protests against the Vietnam war (1965–71). The real threats to America, as I saw it at the time, were the power of the military-industrial complex and the conservative mind-set that supported White Citizens Councils, the John Birch Society, anticommunist hysteria, and segregation. Trying to understand and combat these forces, along with trying to meet my responsibilities as a father and young academic, took most of my time and energy. All of this is to say that there were many complex social and political issues confronting America in the 1960s, and the plight of gay and lesbian persons was not a major issue on my agenda.

Like most of liberal and moderate America, I began to pay attention to gay and lesbian persons when various liberation movements began to surface in the early 1970s. The insights and perspectives of various liberation theologies—black, feminist, third-world—were the intellectual foundations for my pilgrimage toward "new eyes." In that journey I owe much to my deceased mentor at Duke University, Frederick Herzog, who was among the first of America's white male theologians to identify with the plight of oppressed persons. He also introduced me to James Cone, whose early writings stunned me and shook the foundations of my theological world. Meeting Rosemary Radford Ruether at the St. John's University Institute of Ecumenical and Cultural Research in Minnesota in the summer of 1972 was a major factor in stretching my consciousness of feminist theology. The power of Gustavo Gutiérrez's *A Theology of Liberation* (1971) helped me to see how middle class and North American most of my earlier theological and social orientation had been. Collectively these new perspectives helped me see more clearly the ideological components that have shaped the telling of the Christian story. I came to see that there are no self-evident universal truths, and no way of describing the "human condition" that is broad enough to encompass all the variations of gender, race, class, and nationality. Everything in theological discourse depends on *who tells the story, what race or group is regarded as normative,* and *whose experience counts.* Another way to say that is to acknowledge that all theologies are shaped by culture, ideology, and class and gender bias.

A second component of my intellectual pilgrimages grew out of my readings in sexuality as I taught undergraduate and graduate ethics classes. In that work I came to understand how complex human sexuality is, and how narrowly most churches had understood and defined "legitimate" sexuality. James B. Nelson's classic book *Embodiment* (Minneapolis: Augsburg Publishing House, 1978) made an enormous impact on me, so much so that I still regard it as one of the most influential books I have read in my professional career. Feminist perspectives on sexuality from Beverly Wildung Harrison and Carter Heyward underscored the violent and controlling patterns of much of male heterosexual behavior. I learned that the terms "masculine" and "feminine" are properly used, not so much for sharp gender contrasts, as for clusters of traits that are found in varying degrees in all persons. I learned more about bisexuality and about the special issues of sexuality in different ethnic and age groups. I came to understand that sexual norms, like theological systems, are not divinely given, but are shaped by social and cultural influences. The analyses of various feminists helped me see how patriarchal our society has been, and how patriarchy has been such a silent but powerful ideology in our understanding of male-female relationships. The traditional church teachings that only married heterosexual sex is moral and proper did not seem to me to be sensitive enough to speak helpfully to large segments of the human community. Both as a churchman and as a scholar, I was developing "new eyes" with which to comprehend human sexuality, and this gave me a new openness with which to understand gay and lesbian persons.

A number of personal experiences added to my deepening perceptions. When my wife, Mary Charlotte McCall, entered law school in the fall of 1975, she became a part of a group of mature women who were entering law school to pursue second careers. Most were in their thirties. Some of these women were lesbians, and they were accepted and affirmed by the broader group. I came to know them through Mary Charlotte and found them to be bright, winsome, humorous, and intriguing women. Some had been bonded with partners for years. They had broad social concerns for our community and were active in civic life. I liked them all, and came to realize how unrealistic my stereotypes were about lesbians and their life partners.

In 1978 I left Florida State University to serve a college in North Carolina. While living there, I came to know several gay men who took me into their confidence. I sensed their pain and fear of social ostracism. All of these men were responsible professionals and their lives in no way fit the cruel stereotypes that had been perpetrated by the dominant heterosexual society.

In the fall of 1987 I was asked by Isabel Wood Rogers, the Moderator of the Presbyterian Church (U.S.A.), to chair a General Assembly Committee on Human Sexuality. I was reluctant to do so because of time pressures, but I finally agreed. During the following four years the work of that committee took me into hitherto unexplored areas of human sexuality. All members of the committee read widely, listened to national experts, and had our understanding stretched. We came to know others on the committee whose life experiences had been different from our own. We sympathized with the concerns of single people, the elderly, and persons with disabilities. The work of that committee forced me to come to grips with concerns of gays and lesbians in a way that I had not previously been required to do.

During its four years of work the committee met in different cities around the country and held open hearings about human sexuality at General Assembly meetings in Saint Louis (1988), Philadelphia (1989), and Salt Lake City (1990). It became clear that although we could identify many serious problems related to human sexuality, the one driving (and virtually obsessive) concern of most Presbyterians was with gay and lesbian persons. The most sensitive point was whether or not our committee would recommend that such persons be eligible for ordination to any church office (i.e., minister, elder, or deacon). From the beginning I was aware of how emotional and intense this issue was (is); many people felt that the whole future of the Presbyterian Church (U.S.A.) might rest on what our committee said about gays and lesbians. Much in this debate revolved around biblical interpretations and ethical absolutism; there were also apparent issues of power and patriarchy at stake.

I tried to keep the committee on a steady and rational course as we pursued these problems. Two experiences, however, moved me deeply and helped intensify my compassion for gay and lesbian persons. One was the experience of talking with parents who had gay or lesbian children. The "coming out" of their children was usually shocking to them, but they loved these children with the same intensity as their other children, and in no way would they countenance these children to suffer discrimination. These family experiences shattered a lot of myths and stereotypes for the parents, and for me as well.

The other experience came as our committee worshiped with the West Hollywood Presbyterian Church when we met in Los Angeles. (This church ministers predominantly to gay and lesbians persons.) After the service we enjoyed a fellowship meal with the congregation. The Christian commitment of these sister and brother Presbyterians was inspiring. As we visited with the West Hollywood people I sensed afresh how the call of God in our lives transcends sexual orientation.

My responsibilities with the Human Sexuality Committee propelled me into a national controversy after our report was published in March of 1991. I was personally convinced, as were a majority of the members of our committee, that the Presbyterian General Assemblies of 1978 and 1979 had erred when they passed resolutions declaring that no self-acknowledged and sexually active gay or lesbian person should be eligible to be a church officer in the Presbyterian church. I had come to see that God's call to ordination is related to a spiritual calling, to spiritual gifts, and to adequate intellectual ability to complete a master of divinity degree. The call to ordination, in my judgment, is neither affirmed nor negated by one's sexual orientation. I came to feel that human sin, as it pertains to sexuality, is not a matter of sexual orientation but of *exploitation, dishonesty, abuse,* and *violence.* These practices, of course, are found in the heterosexual community as well as in the gay and lesbian communities. Christians speak most helpfully and prophetically when they oppose these practices wherever they are found.

I have learned much in the past twenty-five years about the concerns of gay men and lesbians. Although my intellectual development had been pushing me into new awareness and had been helping me understand the plight of hitherto voiceless and powerless people, it was basically through my personal encounters with individuals that my old stereotypes faded away. Clearly my responsibility with the General Assembly committee forced me to face this issue squarely. I finally did come to see that the plight of gay men and lesbian persons in our society and in our churches is a basic justice issue, and I interpret it as such every time I talk about it. Given the minority status of gay and lesbian persons, this is not a battle that they can win by themselves. For justice to prevail, heterosexuals with "new eyes" must speak and act.

I feel that I have received a "gift of new eyes" through a slow process over the past twenty-five years. It has not been, however, an easy pilgrimage. I had to overcome many social myths and theological assumptions. In my journey I have been consistently helped by my wife, Mary

Charlotte McCall, who has always been ahead of me on these matters; by Tina Pippin, my gifted colleague in the Religious Studies Department at Agnes Scott College; by Beverly Wildung Harrison and Carter Heyward, wise interpreters of feminist ethics; by Sylvia Thorson-Smith and Marvin Ellison, courageous and eloquent colleagues on the Presbyterian sexuality committee; and by James Nelson, whose writings on sexuality have continued to be marked by grace, wisdom, and compassion. It is easier to make a pilgrimage when one is accompanied by gifted and caring friends. It has been a wonderful journey, however, and I am wiser for it.

→ John J. Carey is the Wallace M. Alston Professor of Religious Studies at Agnes Scott College in Decatur, Georgia. He chaired the Presbyterian Church (U.S.A.) General Assembly's Committee on Human Sexuality from 1987 to 1991.

20

One More Hurdle

→ GRACE S. KIM

In 1987 I was asked to serve on the General Assembly Special Committee on Human Sexuality of the Presbyterian Church (U.S.A.). The seventeen members came from different regions of the country and represented diverse theological and racial backgrounds. The majority of the members were ministers and seminary professors. There were four elders, including two physicians; I was one of the elders and the only high school teacher. At the time I was teaching high school courses on family life and personal growth, including sex education. I was surprised and pleased to be selected as a committee member. I am not an expert on human sexuality, although I had worked with high school students struggling with sexual issues.

I grew up in a very conservative Christian environment both in China and Korea. In our family, the moral view on sexual behavior was clear and strict, right and wrong. I had little exposure to or knowledge about homosexuality in my growing-up period. I am happily married, have two sons, and there are no known gays or lesbians among my relatives. Therefore, I didn't have much awareness or opinion regarding homosexuality until I was appointed to the General Assembly committee. I had to educate myself about the issues. I read as many books as I could on the topic.

My three and half years of working with the committee included eye-opening experiences. Not only did we review all previous Presbyterian studies of sexuality, but also we had extensive open hearings throughout the country. We heard widely different perspectives and opinions on homosexuality. We heard a lot of pain, sorrow, anger, and confusion. During the process of deliberation, we shared our own feelings and thoughts about sexuality. We frequently cried and prayed together.

We struggled with our mission. Should our report be prophetic and visionary? Or should we stick to the traditional church teachings that condemn all sexual relations as sinful unless they are between one man and one woman in marriage? How can we address the sexual needs of single

adults—young and old—who make up one-third of our Presbyterian congregations? What do we do with the pain and sorrow of marginalized,
powerless, and ostracized gay and lesbian persons, who represent 8 to 10
percent of the general population? How can we have an open and honest
dialogue with adolescents who are struggling with or confused about
their sexuality?

We were divided in our opinions and theological orientations. But we
all contributed to the process. The majority report, signed by eleven members, including myself, represents a more prophetic and visionary view of
human sexuality. The minority report, prepared by four members, offers
a more traditional, conservative perspective. Two members abstained.

Through my experience as a member of this committee, I learned a lot
about myself, and my thinking and beliefs have changed. This experience
in my faith journey helped me clarify where I stand with regard to the homosexuality issue, and it has deepened my spiritual growth. I see now
that the factors that influence my thinking go back to my roots and personal experiences during formative developmental years. Those early
personal observations of the marginalized and disfranchised, the life of
alien powerless minorities, and the status of women in Asia shaped my
beliefs today.

Korea was occupied and ruled by the Japanese military power for
thirty-six years, until the end of World War II. Because of the Japanese occupation, my grandparents and parents went into exile and moved to
China. Theirs was the first generation to be converted to Christianity by
American missionaries in Korea at the turn of the century. They joined the
underground independence movement in Shanghai, where the Korean
provisional government in exile had relocated.

Thus I was born to Korean parents and grew up in Shanghai. The Korean church in Shanghai was our extended family and the center of Korean people's communal activity. From my young age, I realized that we
were people without a country. Koreans were oppressed and discriminated against as a minority of minorities. I learned about the Korean people's struggle for independence and freedom. I knew that we had to work
hard together to gain independence at whatever cost.

When I started kindergarten in Shanghai, I attended a Japanese school
because Shanghai was already under Japanese government control. We
were asked to change our Korean names to Japanese names. We were for-
bidden to use the Korean language. Japanese classmates and teachers
treated me differently. I played mostly with Korean or Taiwanese children in school. I always felt like an outsider and somehow of a "lower

class" than my Japanese classmates. Some Chinese friends were very friendly and sympathetic with me, but others were somewhat rude. They called me names and made fun of me. I was sad, confused, and angry. I cried a lot. But whenever I went to the Korean church, I felt better, accepted and happy.

We returned to Korea from China after Korea was liberated from Japan at the end of World War II. I felt that in Korea, women were treated not equally, but as second-class citizens. I became more acutely aware of the existence of the Korean social class structure and pecking order: of where poor people, low-class people, uneducated people, handicapped people, and orphans ranked.

When I came to the United States to marry my husband, I recognized the same kind of racial, gender, and class discriminations in this country. I watched as the civil rights movement, headed by Dr. Martin Luther King Jr., brought about significant changes. I felt very excited about these changes.

However, the political climate has changed in recent years. There is a strong movement to do away with multiculturalism and affirmative action. There is growing anti-Asian and anti-immigrant sentiment. Everyday I read more about race-related hate crimes in this country. I am very disappointed and upset that racism is still rampant.

In the high school where I teach, I began to pay more attention to gay and lesbian students. Many brilliant, talented, and gifted young people have come to me and shared their struggles with their sexual orientation. They feared that other friends might hate them, and that their parents would be disappointed. They felt sad, depressed, and confused; some felt suicidal. Some sought psychotherapy and came "out of the closet." A few talked to their parents, and regained their self-esteem and confidence through the love and understanding of their families. Some were rejected by their parents. Some students organized a support group and have helped each other in school. A few are still so fearful that they do not know what to do.

As a member of the General Assembly committee, I met many gay, lesbian, and bisexual people struggling because of their different sexual orientation. I now see that they are not the problem. I now realize that they are very loving and caring Christians. They are genuinely dedicated church leaders and children of God. They are real people, and we heard their pain and struggles in our church.

For the first time I realized how much these brothers and sisters of our loving God are suffering and hurting as a result of our church's policy of discrimination. I began to feel anger in my heart. I made up my mind that I must do something about this injustice. To me, discrimination against gays and lesbians is a social justice issue and a civil rights issue that affects us all.

How long did it take to liberate slaves and grant women's voting rights? How long did it take for the Presbyterian church to accept the ordination of women as ministers? Now there is a powerful political backlash against this civil rights movement. Sexism still persists. Justice for people of all sexual orientations is one more hurdle we need to cross.

After the report of the Special Committee on Human Sexuality was released in 1991, I received many hate letters and even threats because my name appeared as a member of the majority report, which advocated allowing the ordination of gays and lesbians. I also received many supportive thank-you letters. I would like to share parts of two such letters.

Letter from a lesbian teacher

I have been waiting to write to you for several weeks, since I finished reading the report on human sexuality. I sat down with the intention of reading it straight through so that I would be ready to defend it against the attacks that were bound to follow. But I was in no way prepared for my personal response to the committee's findings and recommendations. My first clue to the depth of that response was my inability to read more than a few pages at a time. Then I had to stop—usually to cry. There was so much to take in—so much that touched the wound in me, so much pain and anger and fear. But mostly I cried. Even today I cry—or want to—every time I speak of the report. I have waited decades for those tears; I have waited decades for the church to say, "we are sorry."

I want you to be able to understand why for me the report is not just about justice, or even acceptance—for me the report brings a healing message. . . . The committee's work has given me an opportunity not just for tears, not just for waves of anger, but for healing. Finally, at last, somebody in the church is willing to stand up and say, "We are sorry—we made a mistake. We understand how much we have hurt you."

I think that the church needs to say, "we're sorry for the way in which some Christians have actively persecuted gays and lesbians in the name of God. We're sorry for the way in which most Christians have chosen to witness this persecution silently. We're sorry that the church has placed itself as a wall between gays and God. . . . " And the church needs to be willing to listen to and minister to those gays and lesbians it has hurt, whether or not they are Christians. . . .

I regard sin as something that causes a "hardening of the heart" either in me or in someone else. "Hardening of the heart" is sinful because it makes us less open to give and to receive love—to and from others, to and from oneself, to and from God. I have done things in my relationships with others that I consider sins because they have hurt me and/or others in ways that caused hearts to harden. I also think that learning to lie and to hide was a sin. . . .

When I look at my life, I see that from the time I was sixteen, the vulnerability and strength I have developed through my lesbianism have, for the most part, softened my heart. . . . I know that I am a much deeper person, a much more whole person, a much more Christian person, through my relationship with the women I have loved and who have loved me. . . .

I know that you, and the others who signed the report, did not forget us. So I thank you from the bottom of my heart for this gift of healing which I accept despite the pain it brings. My prayers are with you—so also are my deepest respect and gratitude.

Letter from a Presbyterian minister

I decided to leave the ministry before this couple threatened me to leave if I do not follow what they want me to do. They will publicly announce my sexual orientation. I decided to leave the ministry because of the departure of my partner after eight years of a committed relationship. He was simply fed up with having to lie about our relationship with our closest friends in the church, with deceiving and pretending on a daily basis, and with all of the unhealthy emotional energy we invested in being in the closet.

The trauma and pain of his leaving heightened my awareness of my own growing dissatisfaction with having to live a lie about who I was. I, too, was emotionally weary of having to live under the pretense that I was someone I was not, and that generated an enormous amount of despair and self-hatred. If I was to live with the kind of honesty, integrity, and wholeness that God intended for my life, I realized I could not do so as a Presbyterian minister.

Six weeks later, however, my worst nightmare came true. Toward the end of March this couple sent letters to twenty-five people in our Presbytery informing them that I was gay. What had, up to that point, been private and confidential, was now a matter of public discussion. With the rumor mill being what it is in the church, it would only be a matter of days before the congregation and rest of Presbytery knew who I really was. . . .

I laid awake that night wondering what in the world would happen next? After several sleepless nights I finally did what I had preached about to others so many times. I turned to God and prayed: I am putting this situation, I am putting my life in your hands. I have no control over what will happen next.

As I prayed, I had a vision (I realize it's not very Presbyterian to have visions) of giant loving arms enfolding me. My body was surrounded with warmth and peace. My fear and my anxiety and my sleeplessness left, and I felt a serenity and a confidence I had never before experienced in my life. . . .

With my anxiety gone, and filled with a strength I had never before possessed, I decided it was time to be open and honest. I called a special meeting of the Session, and through a teary and emotional discussion, I told them the truth of who I was, what this couple had done, and why I felt I needed to resign.

The following Sunday I lived through what I always felt would be my worst moment: At an informal gathering of the congregation after worship, I told the congregation that I am a gay man, the circumstances of the last three months, and the reasons why I could not stay as their pastor. Two days later I stood before the Presbytery and told my story a third time. Each time I spoke, I gained power to face the next situation, filled not only with anger, grief, and pain, but also with a new and overwhelming sense of dignity, grace, and gratitude. . . .

The biggest surprise for me through this whole experience has been the response of people to my revelation. I expected anger, hostility, fear, and rejection. Instead I encountered love, affirmation, support, and care beyond my wildest imagination. The Session unanimously supported me. The congregation rose to give me a standing ovation, and exhibited a quality of love and compassion that can only come from God. Thirty-five members of the congregation stood with me in front of Presbytery. Representatives of the Session expressed their support of me, their affirmation of my ministry, and their anger at the denomination which deprives me of continuing in ministry now that I have "come out." . . .

Someday, I suspect, our successors will look back at this time and smile, or perhaps weep, because we were so sexually insecure that we made a particular expression of human sexuality one of the trials for ordination. Someday, I suspect, the Presbyterian Church will overcome its selective biblical literalism and take ever more seriously the central message of the gospel. Someday, I suspect, we will manage to recover our Presbyterian form of government where the decision to ordain or not to ordain is made by the Presbytery out of a direct living relationship with the candidate and not by the mandate of an impersonal policy. Someday, I suspect, we may even get beyond our fear of the way in which love is expressed in a certain segment of our society, so that we may then be free in Christ to become his fully inclusive body. . . .

*The week after I resigned from the church, four church members came by
to see me individually. My coming out to the congregation gave them permission to "come out" to me as they implored me to keep their secret from
other members of the church. Over a dozen others called: people who had a
gay son, or a lesbian aunt or granddaughter, people who said uniformly
that they would never dream of sharing this with anyone in the church because they feared rejection. . . .*

*One of the things I have learned from this whole experience is that while
the church institutionally may have a problem with homosexuality, church
people can love and accept gays and lesbians. That, at least, is a beginning.
As more gays and lesbians in the church experience the transformational
power of coming out, more and more ordinary church people will be compelled to reconcile their prejudices and stereotypes with these flesh-and-
blood individual people who they know and love. . . .*

*My hope and prayer is that before I go to my grave I will be able to re-
claim my ordination to the Word and Sacrament in the Presbyterian
Church (U.S.A.). Not under the current circumstances of "don't ask, don't
tell," where I have to lie, deceive, and pretend in order to be faithful to my
calling. But under the circumstances of openness, honesty, and integrity,
where I can be fully who God has created me to be. . . .*

My own final words: I am grateful to God that some churches are having open and honest dialogue, and some churches are taking courageous
action to declare that they will not consider sexual orientation in accepting members or in nominating, electing, and ordaining any officer.

→ Grace S. Kim is a first-generation Korean American immigrant, a third-
generation Presbyterian, an ordained elder, and a member of Davis Community Presbyterian Church in Davis, California. She taught courses on child development, human development, family life, and personal growth at Davis Senior High School for twenty-four years. Grace has been president of Asian
American Presbyterian Women and chair of the Ethnic Concerns Committee of
the Synod of the Pacific, and she continues to write a weekly column, "Dear
Grace," in the Korean language newspapers in the United States. She is married to Luke Kim, a psychiatrist, and is the mother of two sons.

⇒21⇐

Becoming a Christian

⤳ TRICIA DYKERS KOENIG

No thunder and lightning. No Damascus Road conversion. Baptized at the age of two months, I have never known a time when I did not consider myself to belong to Jesus Christ. But when asked the question, "When did you become a Christian?" I hearken back to several particularly significant turning points in my faith journey.

The first one happened during my high school years in Richmond, Virginia. My congregation was participating in "lay witness mission." During small-group discussion, I remember saying, "I've already accepted Jesus as my Lord and Savior; now I'm just waiting for him to tell me what to do with my life." A man in my group responded, "Hasn't he already told you?"

I started to protest. What I meant was, What am I going to be when I grow up? Does God want me to be a rock star, a famous journalist, a learned authority in . . . ? Then I realized the truth my adult friend was pointing out: God's will for my life had already been revealed in the life of Jesus Christ and I could live out that vocation in any occupation. No waiting was necessary.

I became a Christian.

That lay witness mission was the beginning of an ongoing small-group experience that lasted the rest of my high school days, and I was immensely blessed to be accepted as an equal by adults in my congregation. Yet, I wondered about the warnings some of them gave me as I set off to college: Be careful about religion courses; they might undermine your faith. Pretty flimsy faith, I thought, that could be undermined by being exposed to new ideas.

I went to Duke University expecting to go into political science, but at the end of my freshman year I decided to become a religion major. I am still not sure why I made that decision, based on inner conviction rather than any classroom experiences or career options, but it was the beginning of one of the greatest ongoing adventures of my life: the study of scripture. I had read and studied scripture before, of course, but for the most part with little satisfaction. In fact, the Bible made me feel somewhat guilty—not because it showed me my sin, though that was true enough, but because I never seemed to get from it the same spiritual high that was claimed by my friends in Young Life and other groups. Not wanting to be different, I had feigned excitement, all the while uneasy about my dishonesty, wondering what I was missing and what was wrong with me that I didn't get it. Now, in academic study, I learned a new way to read the Bible, and it changed my life.

Before Religion 52, Introduction to the New Testament, I had a vague idea, though I can't remember ever being taught it, that if the Bible is the Word of God, God must have whispered it to someone way back when; and since God generally does not whisper to me, the Bible seemed unreal, remote, removed from my life. In class, I was thrilled to be introduced to a variety of holy writings that were records of *real* people struggling to make sense of the experience of God in their *real* lives, lives that for all the cultural differences were remarkably similar to my own life when it came to basic issues of faithfulness and meaning. They wrote to help their own communities know God, and know what it meant to be faithful to God in their time and place. I came to understand that God was with them in the same way that God is with me and my community, that we face many of the same fundamental questions that the biblical writers did. The scriptures became alive for me. I fell in love, and I'm in love still.

I became a Christian.

When graduation time drew near, I chose a next step that would allow me to continue doing what I loved: I went to seminary. By that time, I had also grown hungry for intentional assistance in applying what I was learning in class to my faith, an emphasis not present in undergraduate academic endeavors, despite the clear faith of many of my professors. At McCormick Theological Seminary, I was able to continue my studies and also prepare for future employment. As a pastor, I would have the opportunity to share with others the good news about scripture and its message that was bringing such excitement and energy to my life. Some church might actually pay me to have fun doing what I loved!

I became a Christian.

Fast-forward to 1991. The Presbytery of Western Reserve had elected me as a minister commissioner to the 203rd General Assembly of the church in Baltimore. The majority report of the Special Committee on

Human Sexuality, "Keeping Body and Soul Together," had the church in an uproar even before it was published. I read and reread the report, and the minority report, as well as news coverage in the secular and church press. I read the letters I received as a commissioner, some of which I would term hate mail, had I been the target of the invective. I prayed. And as another part of my preparation, I attended two presbytery gatherings designed to afford a large number of persons the opportunity to speak and to listen.

I was shocked. While there were thoughtful, gentle, statements both pro and con, some people who stood to speak against the report, in defense of their understanding of Jesus, seemed to spew venom. On the second evening, a woman sat in the pew behind me, muttering slurs about "homos." I left that meeting literally in tears, grieving that such hostility could be offered as Christian witness. It gave me a small but vivid taste of the suffering experienced by gay men and lesbian women, though at the time I was not consciously aware of knowing any.

As the Assembly approached, I wondered whether I should preach about the report, and the public controversy it was engendering. I was not interested in stirring up controversy in my own congregation, but ignoring what was in the news did not seem responsible either. I turned to the lectionary readings, and once again I heard the call of God: the Gospel lesson was Mark 2:26–3:6, in which Jesus is criticized for plucking grain on the Sabbath. To this criticism Jesus responds: "The Sabbath was made for humankind and not humankind for the Sabbath." I understand that to mean that the law is not an end in itself but a means to wholeness and well-being. Then Jesus violates the Sabbath again, this time by healing a man with a withered hand. In this text Jesus is grieved for the hardness of heart of those who care more for the law than for the welfare of their brother. The message seemed clear to me: If your interpretation of biblical law causes harm, or prevents you from doing good, you had better rethink your interpretation.

"Keeping Body and Soul Together" dealt with many sexuality issues, but it was clear that the lightning rod for the fierce emotional reaction it caused was the report's recommendation that qualified gay men and lesbian women be ordained in the denomination. The General Assembly refused to adopt the report, and also refused some modest amendments to the Pastoral Letter it sent to the church, amendments that would have made the Letter a bit more pastoral toward those who were most hurt by the Assembly's action. What must it be like to bear the brunt of society's fears and insecurities about sexuality? When I tried to imagine how the General Assembly's action must feel to someone labeled "self-affirming, practicing, homosexual person," I was ashamed of my church. The most powerful, Spirit-filled experience of the Assembly for me was the demonstration that followed the vote: a silent witness by grieving Presbyterians of all sexual orientations, punctuated by the sound of nails being hammered into a cross; singing mingled with tears.

I became a Christian.

After General Assembly, I felt compelled to continue the education about homosexuality that I had barely begun. Why, when it came to gays and lesbians, was the church contradicting everything I had ever learned about what it means to love your neighbor as yourself? Was it possible that God was making an exception, or could my instinct about how God intends us to treat one another be supported by further biblical and theological study?

When I applied my college, seminary, and ministerial methods of biblical interpretation to this issue, I discovered no condemnation of committed gay and lesbian relationships, but rather persistent challenges to the barriers that divide and the hierarchies that pretend some people are more worthy than others. I read in the Bible of accepted customs very different from ours today; going "back to the Bible" in the literal way that some people advocate would take us to a world of multiple wives and concubines, in which females are considered the property of males. I read of Jesus' Great Commandments, of how his own living of them offended the sensibilities of the proper, law-abiding folks of his day: welcoming outcasts, confronting the self-righteous, challenging established authority and tradition. I read of Peter's amazement in witnessing the gift of the Holy Spirit to the Gentiles. I read of the early church's struggles to appropriate the principle of radical inclusiveness taught by Jesus and made possible by God's Spirit.

So I continued to read, and I also observed. I saw how some Christians were using the scriptures I love as anything but "good news." I saw how they quoted the Bible to justify prejudice and exclusion. I have seen Christians react to lesbian and gay persons with labels, stereotypes, appeals to fear, emotional abuse, and even physical violence, all the while claiming their actions were sanctioned and even blessed by God. I have seen Christians wrestle with the conflict they experience between our culture's hostility toward persons of minority sexual orientation and their personal relationship with other committed Christian friends and family who have acknowledged being lesbian or gay. I have heard church members say: "I feel their pain; I don't intend to hurt anyone, but the Bible says . . . " To me that sounds like, "I would like to love these neighbors as myself, but God won't let me."

My education included meeting openly lesbian and gay persons and witnessing the deep faith and spiritual gifts evidenced by many of them. I count as one of the great blessings of my life the opportunity I have had to know and work with lesbian and gay Presbyterians whose commitment to Christ and the church keeps them struggling for the church's transformation into greater Christlikeness. Most of us pastors work hard to encourage participation in our congregations. Why, as a church, are we trying so hard to keep some people out, and to discourage their ministries, when against all odds, they join and remain?

I learned that when I display openness, more people are willing to confide in me about their own or their loved one's homosexuality. Whereas I would have guessed that perhaps three families in my small congregation might have gay or lesbian members, I learned there were over a dozen, even before any openly gay folk joined.

I also discovered that some important people in my own life are lesbian and gay. There was the member of my college Christian community, a deacon in the off-campus Presbyterian church most of us attended, who was told by a "Christian" friend visiting him in the hospital that she could not imagine a God who could love a homosexual. There are other classmates from high school, college, and seminary; there are colleagues and parishioners. There are many whose identity must still be concealed, lest they or others be hurt even further by the stigma that my own denomination sanctions.

Each new discovery is further confirmation of a continuing call:

> a call to proclaim that lesbian women and gay men who trust Jesus Christ can live out their vocation and fulfill God's will for their lives without waiting, expecting, hoping, or trying to be changed into heterosexuals;
> a call to share the joy of reading scripture and meeting there a God of grace and love, involved in human lives and continually challenging people to be about discerning the forms that faithfulness takes in new times and places;
> a call to participate in leadership in a community of faith that seeks to ground itself in the good news of Jesus Christ

revealed in scripture, convinced that the news is for all people and that it is exceedingly good; and

a call to join Jesus in standing with those who have been declared to belong outside the bounds of the covenant community.

I am becoming a Christian.

⇥ Tricia Dykers Koenig is copastor of Noble Road Presbyterian Church, Cleve-
land Heights, Ohio, which became a More Light church in 1994, following in-
depth study and dialogue in response to the urging of the 203rd and 205th
General Assemblies. She was a member of the steering committee of Unity
Through Diversity, a joint project of Presbyterians for Lesbian and Gay Concerns and the More Light Churches Network in preparation for the 208th General Assembly.

22

Toward Justice:
A Lawyer's Journey

✦ PETER ODDLEIFSON

My great-great-grandfather was pastor of the Third Presbyterian Church in Rochester, New York. It is said that, during an antislavery rally at Third Church in the 1850s, a woman dared to rise and speak. A woman speaking in church, in violation of clear biblical injunctions, so shocked and dismayed the pastor that he adjourned the meeting and cleared the church. I guess this shows that I have authentic fundamentalist roots!

I went to college in the 1950s at a time when the word "homophobic" was unknown, because everyone was assumed to be homophobic. Until I was forty years old, I did not know that I knew any gay or lesbian persons.

Upon returning to Rochester after law school, I became a member of Third Church and joined a law firm. If anyone had said to me ten years ago that I would become involved in the struggle for the full inclusion of gay and lesbian people, I would have stared at them in disbelief. I was not looking for this issue. My plate was full with professional commitments, community activities, and family responsibilities—but the issue came looking for me.

In 1987, the Brighton Presbyterian Church brought a remedial action against Third Church alleging that, by becoming a More Light church, we had violated church law. Well, being sued does focus one's mind, and I began to think about this problem seriously for the first time.

I had been somewhat active in the civil rights movement during the 1960s and looked upon this lawsuit as another attempt to discriminate against a minority. I realized that I have an obligation to speak out because, as a heterosexual elder, I have no direct personal or economic interest in this issue and, therefore, am in a good position to state the truth as I know it.

And so I agreed to serve on the Committee of Counsel to defend Third Church. During this period, a highly respected member of the session "came out" at an adult education meeting. His honesty about his struggle and his pain moved me deeply. These were two important, defining events for me, and they thrust me into the middle of the controversy.

Defending this case, successfully, through the church courts showed me the harsh, judgmental attitudes that exist in our church. I became aware that this is a major justice issue and that it presented an opportunity for me to confront forces that I believe are destructive and contrary to my own beliefs.

As Presbyterians, we are blessed with a simple faith in Jesus Christ. This is all that is asked of us when we become members. I believe this calls us to love our neighbors, affirm individual dignity, and work for justice in the world. The Greek philosopher Alexander Papaderos described it well: "I came to understand that I am not the light or the source of the light. But light—truth, understanding, knowledge—is there, and it will only shine in many dark places if I reflect it." This spiritual reality requires me to challenge injustice and exclusive, judgmental, demeaning attitudes wherever I find them.

In January 1992, the Downtown United Presbyterian Church called the Rev. Jane Adams Spahr to be a pastor. I remember well the night she stood before presbytery and answered sometimes difficult questions. At one point in the hour-long interrogation, she was asked if she wanted to sit down, and she replied, "No, I want to stand here so you can see me and I can see you." I have admired her courage from that moment on.

The Presbytery of Genesee Valley affirmed the call and was promptly challenged by several congregations and pastors. Again I was asked to be on the Committee of Counsel to defend our presbytery against these charges.

Janie Spahr was ordained prior to 1978, and we thought that she was protected under the "grandparent" clause attached to the 1978 Definitive Guidance of the General Assembly, which stated that the ruling against gay men and lesbians would not affect the ordination rights of those ordained prior to 1978. I will never forget our hearing before the Permanent Judicial Commission of the General Assembly in Dallas. During that afternoon, the commission heard arguments by lawyers for Janie Spahr and Lisa Larges, two highly qualified and gifted individuals ready for installation and ordination. There was a sense of expectancy in the room, the hope that finally justice would be done (the presbytery had twice upheld Janie's call, and the synod judicial commission had overwhelmingly supported it). Our months of preparation were reflected in the extensive oral argument and the briefs. The commissioners asked two perfunctory questions and adjourned the hearing. We thought we had won. When the commission voted against us, we were shocked and bitterly disappointed. I was left with the feeling that they were not listening, that our presentation

had made no impression on them, and that the commissioners were typical of the prevailing attitude in our denomination. How else can one explain the fact that they engaged in no dialogue with us over an issue that
meant so much to Janie and Lisa, and to the church at large?

Out of the ashes of that decision came Janie Spahr the evangelist, and
the national ministry known as "That All May Freely Serve." My partner,
Kay Wallace, and I have worked with Janie in this extraordinary ministry.
We participated in efforts to remove the ordination ban at the 1993 General Assembly in Orlando; more recently, we have joined with our Unity
Through Diversity project colleagues and others developing strategies
and overtures to create a more inclusive church, at the 1996 General Assembly and beyond.

In the course of our work, we have come to know well many gay and
lesbian people who have the gifts of character and leadership that qualify
them for ordained office. Their spirit and determination in their struggle
against an exclusionary church is truly remarkable. They serve as role
models for the rest of us, showing us how to live life with integrity and
honesty in the midst of criticism and adversity.

All of this has caused me to reflect on the present policy of our church,
and I find it incomprehensible for many reasons. First of all, it seems irrational to bar an entire class of people from ordination without ever meeting them. We are told that the Bible requires this ban, but we now know
that more than half of the biblical scholars at Presbyterian seminaries dis-
pute this and are calling for full recognition and support of gay and lesbian people in our church. Furthermore, in every other case, when applying the Ten Commandments or any other standard, we judge people as
individuals on their own merits. Why do we single out gay and lesbian
people for such harsh, judgmental treatment, especially when there is serious disagreement on biblical interpretation? Why should one opinion,
one interpretation, be forced on all others? There is no good explanation,
and it seems to me that to do so does violence to the basic principles of
Christianity.

The medical evidence also demonstrates the irrationality of the ordination ban. In 1973, the American Psychiatric Association removed homosexuality from the list of mental disorders. In 1994, the American Medical
Association reported that emotional disturbance experienced by gays and
lesbians around their sexual identity is due to a sense of alienation in an
unaccepting environment. Aversion therapy is no longer recommended;
rather, gays and lesbians should be made "comfortable with their sexual
orientation" and should "understand the societal response to it." Modern

medicine is telling us that this is not a chosen "lifestyle" but an essential part of one's being.

I have also been perplexed by the jarring inconsistencies in our church policies. We ordain women in spite of the biblical admonition that women must keep silent in the presence of men. We support the civil rights of homosexual persons in society, while at the same time we call the practice of homosexuality a sin and deny gays and lesbians the right to be leaders in our church. We allow heterosexuals to divorce and bless their remarriages, in spite of the clear biblical condemnation of this "sin," even by Jesus Christ (Matthew 5:32). We allow freedom of conscience on the subject of abortion, which means that we ordain people who have committed "murder" in the opinion of some, but at the same time, we do not allow the ordination of those whose only "sin" is that they live together in loving, committed same-sex relationships. We preach the biblical standards of honesty and integrity, and yet the "don't ask, don't tell" policy of our church requires lying and deceit.

The present policy is not only incomprehensible, it is a tragedy for our church as an institution. In the midst of all the poverty and terror and injustice in this world, we are consuming huge amounts of energy battling over a policy that excludes people who wish to serve the mission of our church. It is time to change our policy, reclaim our Presbyterian heritage, and get on with our work to make the world a better place.

But above all, on a personal level, I am angry that my many good friends must live every day with the emotional pain of knowing they are second-class citizens in the church that they love. It is unfair; it is discrimination. When I see their agony and their many talents, which they want to share with our church, I simply cannot turn my back on them, no matter how long it takes for justice to prevail.

What we need is a church that can celebrate individual gifts and recognize substance over form in relationships. Our common life as Christians is rooted in the teachings of Jesus Christ, who calls us to live our lives in loving, loyal relationships. We affirm honesty, integrity, goodwill, commitment, and a caring attitude toward others. We are critical of deception, unfaithfulness, and abusive relationships wherever we find them. We are called to judge all people by these same standards.

Until that day arrives, we can celebrate the fact that we now have an inclusive church community *within* the larger church, where the spirit of love is alive and well. The power and joy of our worship services, the openness within our group, and the many ways in which we care for one another are part of the continuing witness for the whole church of the future. No one can take that away from us.

My hope is that this energy spreads throughout the denomination and leads us toward a new era in which our lesbian sisters and gay brothers will be welcomed as equal partners.

✦ Peter Oddleifson, a graduate of Yale University and the Harvard Law School, is a senior partner in a large Rochester, New York, law firm and former managing partner. He has served as chair of the Board of Governors of Genesee Hospital, chair of the Board of Directors of Hillside Children's Center, and chair of the "Rochester Fights Back" Coalition Against Drugs. Peter is currently an elder at the Downtown United Presbyterian Church in Rochester. He has four married children and nine grandchildren.

23

Justice Is Not
a Programmatic Effort

⤳   HERBERT D. VALENTINE

I begin at the end of my journey. I am convinced there is no unequivocal scriptural prohibition to ordaining homosexual persons. However, there are deeply rooted cultural prejudices that have contaminated our thinking and understanding. I am equally convinced that the institutional church is not prepared to make a decision for or against ordination of gays at this time and that most Presbyterians do not want to be coerced into taking sides. Nevertheless, I also sense that until we move beyond our ecclesiastical obsession with sexual correctness as a measure of fidelity to Christ, we will continue to be paralyzed institutionally. Other denominations have moved to the ordination of gay persons; in particular, I think of the United Church of Canada which, a number of years ago, validated such ordination. In Baltimore, the largest Reform Synagogue has intentionally called an openly gay rabbi, who has a life partner of many years, to be an associate rabbi. Having dealt with the issue decisively, my friends have made it clear that they have moved beyond paralysis and into exciting ministries. I suspect that our churches would have a parallel experience.

For years I have sought understanding and clarity with regard to the issue of the ordination of gay and lesbian persons to ministry in the Presbyterian Church. For the first twenty-seven years of my life, the issue of homosexuality was not on my radar screen; I vaguely perceived it as some kind of aberrant, mysterious practice that had no relevance to me. Like it or not, however, over the past twenty-five years, like most Presbyterians I have gradually been forced to reconcile my cultural contaminations about gays with my faith. I have sought biblical insight. I have sought guidance from the *Book of Confessions,* which I experienced as more culturally biased than I was. The *Book of Confessions* was not particularly helpful on this issue. Furthermore, expanding knowledge in the genetic sciences clearly opens the possibilities of genetic programming of homosexuality. I have had conversations with a professor who is a genetic scientist at Columbia University, and while he told me there is no absolute causal connection between genes and homosexuality, the preponderance of research suggests there is a real possibility of a relationship. I came away convinced that the alleged scriptural warrants against gays are far more tenuous than are the possibilities of genetic linkages. Are we once again replaying the conflict between science and religion? And of course we must consider the reality that gays for centuries have been effective communicators and servants of the gospel. As someone has said to the question, Should we ordain gays? the answer is, Why should we stop now?

Physicists continually seek a "unified theory of creation" and haven't yet found the formula; cosmologists contemplate the beginning and ending of the universe only to find more surprises; theologians and biblical students discover that what they once found immutable isn't and that what was perceived to be precise has become blurry. Just as the great doctors of science and the church are confounded by God's creation, I have come to realize that there are no easy or neat answers to any difficult questions before the church. With all candor, I have been forced to the conclusion that there is no unambiguous guidance that forbids the ordination of gays. All of the frequently used biblical arguments to the contrary torture the scripture. After all the contradictory thinkers have had their say, I am left with the witness of Jesus to guide me, and he doesn't say a word at all on the subject.

So what am I left with? I am given the broad biblical themes. I am convinced that if one seeks understanding with "heart and mind and soul," one must come inevitably to the conclusion that the Bible is undeniably and overwhelmingly for the "outcast" and embraces radical inclusiveness. Carl Sandburg said that the ugliest word in the English language is "exclusive." I must agree. It is inconsistent with biblical imperatives. Justice is another biblical theme that is central for me. It certainly permeates both the Old and New Testaments. The sheer volume of scriptural references on these two themes alone would suggest that they ought not be discounted in the ordination debate.

As a child during the early '40s, I witnessed the forced relocation of my American Japanese playmate and his family during those particularly xenophobic war years. I didn't fully comprehend the magnitude nor the evil of that political act, but as a child I knew innately that my friend was hardly a threat to anyone. I suggest that ordained gays are no more a threat to the church than was my childhood friend a threat to this nation. The memory of that World War II injustice had a profound effect on me.

As Moderator of the 203rd General Assembly (1991), I had the privilege to wear the Moderator's Cross, which had its origin as a gift from a Japanese Christian congregation. They gave a sterling silver celtic cross as a simple yet profound thank-you to the pastor of Fourth Presbyterian Church of Chicago. It was he and that congregation which in the 1940s gave them succor and support when no one else would during that sad part of our national history. That pastor and church received much abuse for their singular act of kindness. That celtic cross has now been riveted to two others as the Moderator's Cross. It is for me a personal symbol of the church's stand against injustice despite popular disapproval. I wore that cross at that Baltimore General Assembly as the gays gave their "silent witness" to the injustices they have suffered. The irony and the appropriateness of my wearing it during that moment in our church's history go beyond expression.

As a teenager I was on a basketball team. I was the only white kid; the others were African American. We were asked to play in a tournament. It was being held at a "whites only" athletic club. We didn't know what we were getting into, but once there, being the only white kid, I was the one told we couldn't play because "niggers" weren't allowed. I had to break the news to my friends. Again the injustice of it all had a profound influence on me. Interestingly enough, it was a Presbyterian church league that later allowed us in.

As a young pastor in my first parish in the early '60s, I was called by the son of one of my elderly parishioners for counseling. He was depressed and grieving deeply. His life's companion and lover of thirty years had died. My seminary training didn't prepare me. My life experiences didn't prepare me. I hadn't any awareness of the gay community or of any support system there. My congregation was of little help, and our national church wasn't even thinking about this subject. Society's oppressive attitudes made it all the more difficult to find help. As I listened to this man's story of the caring relationship he had for so many years, I was overwhelmed by the injustice of it. I was depressed for days. I reflected on the duplicitous life he was forced to live. I didn't like the fact that my church participated in his oppression because of its ignorance and silence. I felt helpless in face of the enormity of the injustice.

These three vignettes are much more intricate and powerful to me than I can relate here. But they all contributed to that sense of justice that permeates my very being. It was that justice value that led me to the church as a place where justice could "roll down" like water. It was in the church that I found people committed to justice. I wouldn't be in the church today if it were not for faith-filled Christians who gifted me with a scriptural framework and a personal witness to the wonderfully inclusive gospel. I get perturbed when I am told that the gay issue before the church has nothing to do with justice. That is the same as telling me that the scriptures have nothing to do with life and that the gospel I believe has nothing to do with my experience.

In the gay ordination debate the victim is often blamed for his or her condition. In the book *Habits of the Heart,* Robert Bellah, Episcopal layman and sociologist, writes of his concern that "individualism may have grown cancerous (in our country) in that it may be threatening to freedom itself." He expands on this theme and suggests that Social Darwinism is on the rise. The implicit and often explicit message is that the deserving survive, the strong get the job done; the weak, the poor, the underclasses, the street people, the gays, the culturally different are that way because of their own actions and deserve what they get. Their existence must be someone's fault—most likely their own. Their culture is defective, their family systems are no good, and so on. It will always be difficult, if not impossible, to give moral meaning to people who do not fit in. In our individualistic society, there is the implicit understanding that cultural misfits are fundamentally illegitimate and therefore outside the pale of caring. Unfortunately, the church has accepted this predominant cultural bias concerning gays and calls it biblical. Yet the debate that is dominating the church clearly suggests that there is more than one way to examine the evidence.

Biblical scholars and theologians have been divided; the academics have been sending out mixed signals about the biblical and theological propriety of ordaining gays. I have assiduously read and listened to numerous persuasive but opposing interpretations. Their think pieces exhibit integrity and have been helpful, but are contradictory and as inconclusive as they are passionate. One book edited by Professor Choon-Leong Seow of Princeton Seminary included chapters written by thirteen members of the faculty; if one simply added up the for's and against's, the for's were more numerous. But that is not the point. People with unassailable scholarly credentials radically differed. In other words, the best of scholarship is unable to offer a rationally convincing case for an absolute "proof text" yes or no if that is what one is seeking. Our seminary think tanks therefore make a de facto case for continuing to talk and continuing to live with and in the midst of ambiguity in these matters.

I know that in these times of upheaval many church people want certainty in particular matters of faith. I suggest that it is OK not to have certitude if those "measures of faith" are not "essential" tenets of the Reformed tradition. I do not believe the ordination of gays deserves such stature. I also suggest that it is OK to live in Christian ambiguity, open to God's continuing revelation, rather than in a closed system that excludes new possibilities. One of my favorite philosophers, the longshoreman Eric Hoffer, puts it this way: "To be in possession of absolute truth is to have a net of familiarity spread over the whole of eternity. There are then no surprises, no unknowns, all questions have already been answered, all decisions made, all eventualities foreseen."

The broader arguments that I have heard have been perhaps less academic but no less passionate for or against ordination of gays. These seem to be rooted more in cultural norms and prejudices than on biblical foundations. That is not to say that biblical language and scriptural quotes are not tossed about. I've heard gays tell their stories with great eloquence and power. Yet I have heard them dismissed out of hand by the pastor of a very large evangelical Presbyterian congregation as being "anecdotal" and thus irrelevant, only to hear this same pastor praise the stories of "saved" gays. In the evangelical church that I attended in my early years, these stories were called "personal testimonies" and they were valued. Are personal testimonies no longer relevant?

The testimony of the scripture and the testimony of gay persons has touched me at my spiritual center. As I have intimated, my spiritual path as a Christian has been and remains for me profoundly about justice. Spirituality and justice are in my experience inextricably bound together. Justice is not something one does apart from spirituality; it is not a programmatic effort. Spirituality apart from justice rings hollow. To follow Christ is not only a faith commitment but an act of spirituality. My experience in exploring the scriptures has propelled me into a belief system that requires that faith and practice be tightly intertwined. Consequently, involvement in the world (a Calvinist concept given form and substance for me at San Francisco Theological Seminary) is not optional but imperative.

To work in the world and all its subsets (including the ecclesiastical) is to confront monumental injustice in every avenue of living—from the interpersonal to the political to the systemic. As a Christian seeking to find a balance wherein the inner life bears some resemblance to the outer life, and the reverse, this means for me living in the often uncomfortable tension between two kingdoms, the one we are in and the one which is to be. My compulsion to live life in this binary fashion—both as a part of the world and apart from the world—has not been easy nor always a lot of fun. It has never been boring.

I come to this point in my story not because this is where my faith/spiritual journey began or for that matter ends. It is where I am today by virtue of biblical imperatives and life experiences. I have witnessed the excitement, power, and witness of the gospel in lives of people. If I ignore that living and gutsy testimony, I do so at my spiritual peril. There is no doubt in my mind and heart that Jesus brings salvation.

Eugene Peterson's translation of the New Testament (Luke 7:18–23) reads:

> The men showed up before Jesus and said, "John the Baptizer sent us to ask you, 'Are you the One we've been expecting, or are we still waiting?'" . . . Then he gave his answer: "Go back and tell John what you have just seen and heard: The blind see, the lame walk, lepers are cleansed, the deaf hear, the dead are raised, the wretched of the earth have God's salvation hospitality extended to them. Is this what you were expecting? Then count yourselves fortunate!

I count myself fortunate because I have seen the reality of that salvation in the lives of homosexual people.

⤺ Ordained in 1960, Herbert D. Valentine pastored inner-city congregations in San Francisco and the Midwest. He is the Executive Presbyter of Baltimore Presbytery, where he has served for twenty-one years. He was elected moderator of the 203rd General Assembly, Presbyterian Church (U.S.A.) in 1991. He has served on its General Assembly Council and Office of the General Assembly. He was cited by the governor of Maryland for his work in affordable housing. He has been honored for his statewide ecumenical leadership, and is an organizer and national Founding President of The Interfaith Alliance. He also maintains an active involvement with the indigenous presbyteries in Guatemala.

24

What God
Has Called "Good"

✦   NORM POTT

I began as your average born-again homophobic white male. The words "fag," "fairy," and "queer" were part of the vocabulary of my high school friendship circle before I knew what they meant. Once during college years when I was taking a $24 flight from Newark to Chicago, a man next to me started fondling my leg. I was wedged into the seat and couldn't move, and muttered something like "no thanks" while pushing his hand away. My reaction was a combination of shock, fear, anger, and disgust, or in other words, the basic ingredients for homophobia. I could under-stand how a woman could prefer to do it with women; I found women mysterious, beautiful, and irresistible myself. But I could not understand or accept men doing it with men. I've never felt anything close to a sexual attraction for a man.

What began to eat away at my homophobia was the gospel. Coming out of an evangelical Presbyterian family and church experience, and as a Bible major from Wheaton College, I was tuned in to the latter part of John 3:16: "that whosoever believeth in him should not perish, but have ever-lasting life." But four years in the early '60s in Berkeley, and after that, eleven years in Eugene, Oregon, awakened me to the initial words of John 3:16: "God so loved the world." Inspired by God's validating love for each and every human being, I became an active participant in the civil rights movement. Following Martin Luther King Jr.'s analysis of Vietnam as an example of geopolitical racism, I became a protestor against the war in Southeast Asia. Throughout this time I was growing in my ability to welcome all people, to accept all people, to listen, to grant the freedom to others to be themselves, and to resist the rush to judgment if someone practiced something that differed from my way of life.

Still I had not known the experience of personal friendship with an out gay or lesbian person. Their presence in the world came home to me in the '70s as the church began to address the issue of ordination in the months leading up to the General Assembly in 1978. One of the great old war-horses of Sacramento Presbytery, Merrill Follansbee, was dealing personally with a gay son. Out of that experience he provided leadership to the presbytery in awakening many of us to the reality of gay and lesbian persons in this society. I particularly remember a Saturday conference to which Merrill had invited a number of out gay and lesbian persons, and in the interests of equal time, a few "former" gay and lesbian persons who claimed to be converted through the power of Christ from a homosexual to either a heterosexual or celibate way of life. Listening to these people, I found myself resonating with those who had come to an acceptance of themselves as gay or lesbian. For them this was the sexuality that God had given, and in response to God they were committed to making the most of it. In general their relationships seemed much less stable and much more promiscuous than I would have liked, but given the total lack of support from the society and often from their own families, I began to appreciate the particular obstacles they faced. I have also recognized in retrospect that I was comparing actual homosexual expression to idealized heterosexual expression, and not factoring in the glaring distortions and shortcomings that are apparent in heterosexuals. And we all live by grace anyway, right?

I was much more troubled by those who claimed to have been converted from a homosexual lifestyle. Given the plasticity of the sexual continuum, I am prepared to acknowledge that some people in the power of Christ could be led from what appears to be homosexuality to what appears to be heterosexual behavior. But I have not heard of such transitions outside of a perspective that condemns all homosexual expression up front, as being contrary to scripture and in opposition to the will of God. This judgment continues to be promoted in spite of the experience and now the official policy of the medical community: Homosexuality is no longer to be regarded as a pathology; treatments intended to change gay people into straight people are no longer to be regarded as viable. Thus the smiles of skepticism with which gay people react to these conversion stories. From then until now these testimonies of conversion have impressed me as examples of persons who have been motivated to harmonize their behavior with the conservative-evangelical judgment that all expression of homosexuality is sin, rather than as examples of a true reckoning with sexual orientation. Self-affirming gay and lesbian persons know for themselves the impossibility of changing, and they have found Jesus not as a power to change what they are, but as the far more profound empowerment to accept themselves as they have been created. Would that the Presbyterian church could find that empowerment that leads to acceptance!

Since 1978, however, the Presbyterian Church (U.S.A.) has officially embraced the mythology that "unrepentant self-affirming practicing homosexuals" must either be converted to a heterosexual lifestyle or else become celibate in order to be considered eligible to be ordained. By this time on my own journey, primarily through these opportunities to meet gay and lesbian persons and to hear their stories, I was persuaded that the General Assembly was presenting tragic evidence of what is, thank God, a historic principle of Presbyterian polity, "that all synods and councils may err."

The theological prop for the 1978 Definitive Guidance is the assertion that homosexuality is not what God had in mind for the human race but is rather an expression of the Fall. But if homosexuality for some people is a given reality that is not chosen and cannot be changed, then to describe it as an expression of the Fall leads us to the theological dead end where God is the creator of constitutionally compromised human beings. This cannot stand up to the basic assumption of creation theology that God does not make junk.

Furthermore the 1978 Definitive Guidance assumes that homosexual persons can be converted to heterosexuality, and failing that, requires them to become celibate in order to be acceptable. This is an irony in a church that emerged out of the Reformation and endorsed its vehement rejection of celibacy as a requirement for ordination. Not only should we be suspicious of the sudden promotion of a new Presbyterian celibacy, but we should be especially wary of a celibacy that is prescribed by one group for another. The scriptures do not communicate any teaching of Jesus on same-sex relations, much less the phenomenon of homosexuality, but they are crystal clear on his condemnation of people who impose burdens upon others which they themselves are unwilling to bear.

All of this contributed to the profound grief that I felt following the adoption of Definitive Guidance in 1978. However, the experience of friendship with gay and lesbian persons which occasioned the grief has also nurtured the hope that one day the church will receive the gift of their full participation.

Scott Anderson in 1978 was a student at the University of California at Davis and a regular participant in Davis Community Church where I served as pastor. In fact Scott was an advisor to our high school youth group and took a number of them to attend the 1978 General Assembly in San Diego. When I arrived in Davis in 1975, Scott at the age of sixteen was serving as the chair of the Church and World Committee of Sacramento Presbytery. Later Scott shared his conviction of being called to ordained ministry, and he began the process of candidacy in the presbytery. While a student at Princeton Seminary he served along with William P. Thompson as our Presbyterian representative on the governing board of the National Council of Churches. After forty-two years of experience as a pastor in four presbyteries, I see Scott as among the three or four most impressive candidates for ministry that I can remember. At the time I did not realize that Scott was a gay man. From conversations since, I know that he was struggling throughout this time to understand and appreciate his own sexuality. I do remember talking with my associate pastor regarding her dream, which was shared by other mothers in the congregation, that Scott would marry her daughter, and their frustration with Scott's apparent indifference.

Scott's promise was fulfilled following graduation when he returned to Sacramento Presbytery as the pastor of the North Highlands Presbyterian Church. It was a proud and happy day when he invited me to be the preacher at his service of ordination. From North Highlands Scott was called to Bethany Presbyterian. It was there in 1989 that a disturbed person, after Scott refused to give him carte blanche to promote his obsessive doctrines in the congregation, exposed Scott as gay. Scott had near unanimous support in his session and congregation, and I believe that if he had chosen to fight this battle, he could have prevailed. But at the time he was close to exhaustion from the effort to preserve his personal integrity and simultaneously to fulfill his calling as a pastor, and he was determined not to allow himself to be the catalyst for division in the church. After much soul searching he voluntarily resigned his pastorate and with it his ordination.

Scott Anderson is the living evidence of the current folly of the Presbyterian Church. The official position of the church, which was designed by sincere, well-intentioned people to preserve our peace, unity, and purity, has instead compromised the gospel in the eyes of countless people and compelled us to reject someone who has so obviously been called and gifted by God for pastoral ministry. Scott remains a pastor without the confirmation of his community, and he is currently serving as the director of the Office of Church State Affairs, an ecumenical agency relating to the State of California Assembly. The church does not deserve the wisdom and grace of Scott's leadership as he continues year in and year out in the effort to achieve justice and the full inclusion of our gay and lesbian brothers and sisters. I have found nothing more inspiring than this friend's refusal to give up on the Presbyterian church.

Another formative experience for me occurred in the spring of 1992 when Janie Spahr's call to the Downtown Presbyterian Church in Rochester was being challenged by a minority in Genesee Valley Presbytery. In 1985 I had become the pastor of the First Presbyterian Church, San Rafael, where Janie, prior to my time, had served on the staff as an associate pastor. She had been the inspiration and energy behind a highly successful high school youth group and had become a kind of legend in her own time within the congregation. Even people who were troubled about ordaining gays and lesbians were in awe of what Janie had accomplished and could not help responding to her personal charisma and compassion. The session of the San Rafael church was motivated to express its support for Janie as she faced the prospect of a judicial challenge to her call to Rochester in the courts of the church.

We drafted an overture of support which was discussed and voted upon by the session before being forwarded to Redwoods Presbytery. There was one dissenting vote, and this woman shortly thereafter resigned from the session and left the church. Another elder, Dinah McClure, approached Sher, our associate pastor, following the session meeting. Dinah acknowledged the shock in learning in the course of the session's process that the ban against ordaining gay and lesbian persons applied to elders and deacons as well as ministers of the Word and Sacrament. "Did you know that I am a lesbian?" she asked. "Should I resign from the session?"

No, neither Sher nor I had known that Dinah was a lesbian. There was nothing in either her appearance or behavior that would indicate this. We knew her as a single woman and a night nurse at Marin General Hospital. A peripheral friend of the congregation through the years, she had recently become a regular attender and a participant on the Mission Commission, which was the launching pad for many of First Presbyterian Church's ministries out into the community. With a deepening appreciation for the church's role and out of a developing relationship with Sher and others, Dinah had decided to take the plunge of membership, even though her night shift job made it difficult for her to attend many of the church's programs and events. Dinah's commitment and contribution had so impressed her friends, particularly on the Mission Commission, that they had promoted her to the nominating committee as a candidate for elder. Though hesitant because of her job and schedule, she had consented, and at the time of our overture in support of Janie Spahr, Dinah had emerged as the most gifted and dedicated chair of the Mission Commission that we had known, and this on a commission that through the years had been consistently blessed with great leadership.

Dinah's question about resigning was one of the easiest that I have ever had to answer. I think I chuckled and said, "Are you kidding?" but my longer official answer would go something like this: "If you were to resign, it would give credibility to the Presbyterian Church's decree preventing gay and lesbian persons from serving through the ordained offices of the church, but you yourself, your presence and your ministry among us, is the clearest possible indication that the Presbyterian Church is in error. It is the same ignorance and fear that forces gay and lesbian persons to hide their sexual orientation, that has led the church to interpret scripture, to articulate doctrine, and to formulate polity, in ways that deny to homosexual persons the rights and privileges of full membership in the Christian church. In the conviction that we are preserving the purity of the church we have obscured the gospel; we have placed barriers in the way of Jesus' ministry to a whole group of persons."

At this point I can hear someone raising the question, "Yes, but is Dinah a self-affirming, practicing homosexual person?" I am not sure how Dinah would have answered that question. There was a time when most of my gay and lesbian friends would have responded, "Yes: I affirm myself. I am a sexual human being. I express who I am." But now that the Presbyterian Church has used these words officially to define a sinner, most of my Presbyterian gay and lesbian brothers and sisters take the position that if the church insists upon this label to identify a sinner, they are not conscious of themselves as chronic sinners, and therefore they reject the label.

Of course heterosexuals would never say that to be a self-affirming practicing heterosexual is by definition sinful. Rather we would be concerned about the quality of relationship, and whether the sexual expression is healthy, caring, and mutually beneficial, or whether it is exploitative, self-serving, and harmful. Why can't we apply the same sexual ethic to homosexual persons: Why do we judge heterosexual persons for the manner in which they choose to express their sexuality, but judge homosexual persons if they choose to express their sexuality at all?

Dinah makes much more sense to me than the definitions of the Presbyterian Church. She accepts herself as a lesbian woman. She receives her sexuality as a gift from God, and expresses herself in ways that promote mutual enjoyment and positive, enduring relationships. We can be certain that her sexual life is not perfect any more than that of any of the rest of us, but I am also convinced that Dinah McClure's sexuality is nothing that needs to concern the Presbyterian Church. What we need to be concerned about in the Presbyterian Church is that we are continuing to call "unclean" what God has created and called "good."

One outcome of the San Rafael session's support for Janie Spahr was a six-month inquiry into the possibility of becoming a More Light congregation. The primary venue for this was the Adult Study Hour following worship on Sunday morning. We searched the scriptures, read the literature, we heard from gay and lesbian leaders, and once again we heard from people who claimed to be converted away from what was called the "homosexual lifestyle." Attendance swelled at Adult Study. I have never seen the educational quotient of a congregation at a higher point.

For me, however, the unanticipated result of opening this issue was the encouragement that it gave to our gay and lesbian members to come out and to share their experience with us, as well as to many of our straight members to acknowledge children, brothers, sisters, other close friends and relatives who were gay. In actuality we were not so much voting to include some group agitating from the outside as to include a group that was already a part of us, though largely closeted.

At the end of this process the session adopted a statement of inclusion: We would welcome everyone into the church regardless of sexual orientation. We would claim the freedom provided by our church's constitution to elect our own leaders without making sexual orientation a factor in the decision-making process. We would exert ourselves and utilize our resources to eliminate the national church's policy against the ordination of active homosexual persons, including collaborative efforts with other More Light congregations. As a concession to the dissenters within our community, however, the session stopped short of accepting the "More Light" label for ourselves. We laughingly refer to ourselves as "semi-dim." Perhaps the day will come when we will be ready for more light.

An immediate product of this decision in a congregation of more than five hundred members was the loss of a few members, fewer than ten that I am aware of. We lost them on both sides of the issue, a few who objected strongly to the inclusion of gays, and a few on the other side who saw in our refusal to become a More Light church a foot-dragging compromise.

The long-term result is that gay and lesbian people in the congregation have become a non-issue. They are a part of our church family. We have benefited and learned from their experience. In fact there is virtually no "them" anymore. We are all "us." We cannot contemplate a church without these brothers and sisters. Many, like Dinah, have been magnificent leaders. It has become impossible in the face of this contribution for anyone to make a case against the ordination of gay and lesbian persons at First Presbyterian Church, San Rafael.

One of the most outspoken dissenters at the time of our More Light process has—I am thankful to say—remained in our community, and even she says that she is now open to the ordination of gay and lesbian persons as elders and deacons, "but not as pastors," she quickly adds. Of course this is less than a Reformed view of ordination, but it is more than an incidental change in this woman, considering where she was just a few years ago. She has come to the point where she can only say yes to real people who are obvious believers called by God to serve in and through the church.

I look forward to a day that is surely coming when the church as a whole will finally be able to say yes.

↣ Norm Pott is the pastor of the First Presbyterian Church, San Rafael, California, and a member of the adjunct faculty at San Francisco Theological Seminary. In 1996 he was endorsed by Redwoods Presbytery as a candidate for Moderator of the 208th General Assembly of the Presbyterian Church (U.S.A.), and he campaigned for the freedom and responsibility of governing bodies in the church to discern calls, and elect, ordain, and install leaders without discrimination on the basis of sexual orientation.

"Facing" the Issue

✦ SYLVIA THORSON-SMITH AND MICHAEL D. SMITH

Homosexuality. Heterosexuality. Bisexuality. Transgendered. Gay. Straight. Where are you? Where are we? Places on a continuum? *People in relationship.*

For the two of us, this is has been a journey peopled with many faces. It has been an amazing coming-to-awareness that has made us alive to the gifts of other people and, in turn, alive to a better understanding our own selves. Our journey has two roads—two past histories that have brought us together in a shared adventure.

Sylvia's Journey

I grew up in Anchorage, Alaska, nurtured by devout parents who clearly made the connections between believing and doing. My parents "got it"; they understood that the growing civil rights movement of the 1950s was born out of people's lived experience of Christian faith. In our family discussions, I heard them talk about "unfairness" and "compassion" and "the love of Jesus for everyone." I saw them act on their values in several public situations. Now, I have more language for addressing issues of racial justice; then, all I knew was that my parents had a strong faith, and I could see it reflected in the very real ways they expressed their conviction that all people deserved full human dignity.

In the mid '60s I married a Presbyterian seminary student, graduated from college, and moved to Detroit, where my husband had a fifteen-month internship and I worked for an inner-city program that was part of President Johnson's "War on Poverty." In the urban crisis of that time and place, I came face to face with economic injustice and racial discrimination. I also came face to face with my own economic and race privilege. The "riot of 1967," or "rebellion" as I have since heard it named, gave me new eyes—for recognizing my own advantage (I could watch the billowing smoke of ghetto fires from my apartment on the edge of the city) and my own commitment to putting myself in the middle of the struggle (the program where I worked was the first in the area to reopen, even under continuing sniper fire). Not only "an issue" for me, these events had a human face, that of Mary, my friend, who was denied housing when she called about an apartment and was not allowed to swim in a "whites-only" pool. How could I not come face-to-face with the disparity between my white-skin experience of privilege and her black-skin experience of discrimination?

Then there was Minot, North Dakota, and five years of life on the prairie. Far from what might be imagined as a peaceful rural interlude, it was a time of increased social awareness and mounting protest toward an unjust war, environmental abuses, overpopulation, overconsumption, and, increasingly to the forefront, sexism. For me, the first faces of the women's movement were the members of a small ecumenical group that started reading feminist books together. As we did, we told the truth about our lives, supported one another, and started to make more connections. We began to explore the fabric of injustice and see evidence around us of the historic diminishment of women. We examined our lives and our relationships, including those with the church, and we were disturbed and angry at much of what we saw. I looked in the mirror and saw my own face, the face of a woman who was recognizing the limits of personal freedom and the power of social constraint in her own life. I began to understand how institutions can both bind and free people by their policies and corporate practices. I began to experience the power of liberation, of breaking the silence and finding my own voice as a woman.

All this time, I was a minister's wife—a minister's wife who had become an ardent feminist. How could the two go together? What was the relationship between feminism and Christianity? I am grateful that I was a member of the United Presbyterian Church in the U.S.A. My denomination responded to the voices of women, repudiated sexism, and established councils and committees to advocate justice for women in both church and society. I moved to Wichita, Kansas, in 1974, and there I became a member of my presbytery's task force on women; at the same time, I started to earn a graduate degree in sociology and women's studies. I read feminist theology and grew stronger in my conviction that the God of the Bible creates both women and men in the divine image, denounces all manner of injustice, breaks down barriers, and opens the way to freedom.

I saw the face of feminism in many people who supported my journey, but I cherish one very special person, a minister named Bruce, who widened my vision and turned me in the direction of those whom I'd previously not seen and known. To my amazement, this clergyman understood the grip of sexism on the church, interpreted the Bible in new and liberating ways, preached sermons on texts about women, and even talked about sexuality from the pulpit. Bruce, who was on the staff at our church, became my best friend; I loved him for what he gave me as a person and as a woman: a sense of dignity, respect, and value. But he gave me much more than that; he gave me his trust and the revelation that he was gay. With the gift of his own identity, Bruce provided me with one of the most valuable insights about the connections I had been making—he gave me the beginning of an awareness that we can best know *who we are* and *whose we are* when we recognize and affirm the diversity of God's good gift of human sexuality.

Bruce gave me one more priceless gift: an introduction to his good friend Virginia Davidson, from Rochester, New York. Ginny spoke at our church in Wichita when she was Vice-Moderator of the General Assembly, and our friendship deepened over the years through mutual advocacy of women's issues in the church. When she chaired the General Assembly Task Force on Homosexuality, 1976–1978, Virginia Davidson became for me the face of courage, caring, and faithfulness to the gospel of Jesus Christ. For twenty years, she has been a model of what it means to be a "het" ally (a heterosexual ally) in solidarity with gay, lesbian, bisexual, and transgendered persons.

My life in the 1970s and '80s was filled with the faces of lesbians and gay men. Some were faculty and students in the women's studies program at Wichita State University, where I taught. Some were gay and lesbian church members, including ordained elders and clergy, whom I met all over the country as I served on the General Assembly Council on Women and the Church (COWAC), other task forces and committees. I got to know them as colleagues and friends, and I discovered that we are all simply human beings who happen to have different sexual orientations. Some of us have same-sex partners; some of us have partners of the other sex. But we each work, play, worship, love, and live our lives as ordinary people do.

I was divorced, and later married Mike Smith, whom I met on COWAC, who shares my passion for feminism and social justice. We moved to Grinnell, Iowa, in 1986 when Mike became pastor of the First Presbyterian Church, and I subsequently began teaching courses in religious studies and sociology at Grinnell College. Then came 1988 and my appointment as a member of the General Assembly Special Committee on Human Sexuality.

For three years, the seventeen of us studied a whole range of sexuality issues, including the status of lesbians and gay men in the church. More people put a human face on these issues: Marvin Ellison, Dan Smith, Janie Spahr, as well as many members of the West Hollywood Presbyterian Church in Los Angeles and the Downtown United Presbyterian Church in Rochester, who on many occasions have welcomed me into their justice-seeking communities. Countless gay men and lesbians testified before the sexuality committee in closed hearings and "came out" of the closets in which the church compels them to hide. They risked being identified, told the truth about their lives, and challenged us to "love kindness and do justice." In their faces, I made the most important connection of all—that theirs was the face of Christ, calling the church to "set at liberty those who are oppressed," especially those whom the church itself oppresses.

When it came time to write our report, the majority of us knew what we were called to say to the church. It was with the deepest faith conviction I have ever known that I helped write "Keeping Body and Soul Together: Sexuality, Spirituality, and Social Justice." But it was not easy. We were pressured by many throughout the church *not* to advocate a justice-loving ethic of sexuality for people of all sexual orientations and a policy that allowed for the ordination of gays and lesbians. When we stood firm and the report was published, we were targeted, vilified, and labeled heretics. One of our members, an African American woman, lost a presbytery job because she would not renounce her stand in favor of the report. I have a file of letters: one person wrote, "You will not be in hell for long before you realize how wrong you are," but many more expressed appreciation similar to that of one of my former students who wrote: "I am *so* proud of your efforts and commitment. . . . I learned so much about myself as a gay person and a religious/spiritual person in the affirming way you present gays and lesbians and the church."

Since 1991, I have had the pleasure of traveling throughout the church and speaking on issues of human sexuality. In 1993, I was asked to write *Reconciling the Broken Silence*, a widely used study resource on issues related to the status of gays and lesbians in the church, and I have participated in many forums as an advocate for the full rights and privileges, including ordination, of gay and lesbian members. There have been many more people on my journey and many more faces who have expanded my understanding of sexual justice in church and society. A close friend talks to me about her bisexuality; a new acquaintance tells me what it means to be a transgendered person. I am increasingly humbled by the mystery of human sexuality. I am also emboldened to share what I know: that the love of God embraces us all and empowers us to make the connections, in our understanding of faith and life, and in our relationships with one another.

Mike's Journey

The issues came first, then the faces. Now they are inseparable. For me, the issue of sexual orientation began as another justice issue coming on the heels of civil rights and women's issues. My involvement in each movement has necessitated making many decisions about strategy, timing, coalitions, and tactics which have been anything but clear and simple; however, I regard each of these human rights issues, and the people affected by them, as part of the call to struggle for God's justice.

I understand God's passion for justice in the Bible as a matter of righteousness, or right-relatedness, between ourselves and God, and between ourselves and our neighbors. God's justice calls us to relate to each other in the spirit of fairness, equality, and sisterly/brotherly love, as all of us are beloved children of the same good Creator. Justice, or right-relatedness, is measured by God's intent for the good creation, by God's shalom, and by God's free gift of grace and love in Jesus Christ. God not only acts with steadfast love, justice, and righteousness in the earth, but delights in these things (Jeremiah 9:24). God invites us to join in this delightful activity.

Who I am as a person of faith has been shaped most significantly by my participation in struggles for justice. The first was in Selma, Alabama, in March of 1965. It was my senior year at San Francisco Theological Seminary. Some sixty of us decided to charter a bus and head south to Selma, where seminary president Theodore A. Gill and others had already gone in the wake of the terrible beatings of African Americans seeking to gain their voting rights. An excellent seminary education had left me nonetheless with many uncertainties about my faith and future in the church. Much of this conflict, between faith and life, "came together" for me in Selma.

The biblical call to do justice, the issue of civil rights, and the awareness of God's presence in the struggle came together because I had the opportunity to come together with the faces of real people in Selma. The movement of African Americans for justice was clearly rooted in their faith, and their faith was contagious. In those few days of face-to-face experience with victims of beatings who could not be beaten in their struggle for justice, and who reached deep into their trust in Jesus Christ for strength to carry on, I was changed. Theology became more than theory, and civil rights more than an issue. Faith had a face—in fact, it had many faces. Jesus Christ, and God's call to love and justice, became as real as the people of Selma, Alabama. I saw the Christian faith being lived in a way that empowered me to begin living it too.

During the last half of the '60s and early '70s, I was a campus minister in Colorado and Wisconsin and participated actively in efforts to end the war in Vietnam. At the beginning, it was primarily an intellectual and theoretical concern about peace and justice, but very quickly the war took on a human face to me. Vietnamese faces entered our living rooms on television screens, and the lives of more and more Americans became directly affected by the war, including those young men who availed themselves of our draft-counseling ministries.

The movement with the most direct link for me to the issues of sexual orientation has been the women's movement. Once again, it was my concern for God's justice that led me to become an advocate for justice for women. At the outset, abortion was a key issue because, in the '60s and '70s, women regularly looked to ministers for counseling regarding unplanned pregnancies. I was now a campus minister at the University of Arizona in Tucson, participating in a clergy counseling service organized by Planned Parenthood of Southern Arizona before abortion was legalized there. The much-debated issue of abortion had very human faces for me—the faces of women who struggled with difficult decisions in very real lives and circumstances. My experience led to strong support of the Presbyterian Church's position that women possess the God-given ability to make moral decisions, and that the church should protect their right and freedom to make decisions regarding the continuation or termination of their pregnancies.

My active participation in the movement for women's rights has been a profoundly spiritual journey for me, and I have found many opportunities for involvement in the context of my faith. I served on the General Assembly's Council on Women and the Church (COWAC) from 1979 to 1987, presbytery and synod women's advocacy committees in the 1980s and '90s, and General Assembly's Advocacy Committee on Women's Concerns from 1992 to 1994. Along with a deepened commitment to issues of human status and well-being has come a broadened understanding of many social justice issues, including issues of human sexuality.

Sylvia mentioned in her story that we met during our COWAC tenure and were married in 1985. We have had, and continue to have, the joy of learning and growing together while sharing in the church's struggle with its attitudes and policies regarding sexuality. Life has been anything but dull for me, having a marriage partner who coordinated the denomination's study of pornography and served on its Special Committee on Human Sexuality. This does not conform to everyone's image of the typical minister's wife! Over the last decade, our awareness of the need to make connections between all human rights issues has led us increasingly in the direction of seeking justice in the church and society for gay, lesbian, bisexual, and transgendered persons. Here, as with other issues, the more we've been engaged in the effort, the more faces of people we've come to know and love.

Some of the faces on this issue live in Grinnell, Iowa (our home since 1986), and some are active in the two-hundred-member First Presbyterian Church I serve as pastor. These past ten years have included times of great joy and deep caring and times of struggle and conflict, particularly over the issue of sexual orientation. In 1991 we engaged in a study of the Special Committee on Human Sexuality's report to General Assembly. Our church in Grinnell is like most, if not all, churches; some members were eager to discuss issues related to human sexuality and other members preferred not to engage in such study. Our congregation had the whole range of reaction to the General Assembly report, and one group of members hoped we would not have to deal with sexuality issues again.

In 1993 when the General Assembly reaffirmed its policy declaring homosexual practice a sin and a bar to ordination, and also called for a three-year study and dialogue on the issue, the tension in the congregation increased. Some agreed with the policy decision but did not want to talk about these matters any more. Others disagreed with the decision, yet welcomed the opportunity for a more thorough examination of the issues than we had had in 1991. The session voted to engage in study and dialogue, a committee designed a process, and those who chose to participate did so in weekly sessions that lasted several months. Few members who opposed the ordination of gays and lesbians participated in the study and dialogue. As a result, there has not been a thorough dialogue between many church members who hold different views, and conflict remains largely avoided, unresolved, but simmering. Many members still ask the question, Why do we have to keep talking about these issues?

It's not that the issues won't go away; the faces won't, because the faces belong to real people present and among us. Our church has been blessed with the presence and involvement of several active gay, lesbian, and bisexual members, but one woman has done the most to put a human face on these issues. Barbara has been a member of the church and also its music director since 1977. She is a lecturer in music at Grinnell College, where she teaches piano and is staff accompanist. For both Sylvia and me, Barbara has become one of our closest and dearest friends. Committed Christian, gifted musician/artist, and treasured colleague, Barbara is also a lesbian. She lives with her partner of many years and is "out" to her children, friends, and college community, yet Barbara is still not able to be fully who she is in her church community. It is terribly painful for her and for me, and it is terribly wrong. Our denomination's official policy holds that sexual activity between two men or two women, even though expressed lovingly and in a committed and faithful relationship, is sinful. Because I know Barbara and her partner, I know that this policy is wrong. How can I *not* continue to participate in the struggle for sexual justice when I know that Barbara and others like her are the very real people affected unjustly by our exclusionary policies?

Many other "glbt" people have played crucial roles in my journey. Since 1994, I have been a member of the national Executive Board of Presbyterians for Lesbian and Gay Concerns (PLGC). It is a vital part of my ministry to work and witness with these dear friends who put such delightful human faces on the issue of sexual orientation. I simply have not experienced any group more committed to Jesus Christ and the Presbyterian Church, more hard working, more creative, more fun, or more loving than my PLGC brothers and sisters. At the same time, I know of no other people more maligned, more hated, more feared, more rejected, or more discriminated against in the church today than my lesbian and gay friends.

On an airliner traveling to a PLGC meeting in 1995, I composed a paraphrase of chapter 13 of 1 Corinthians that I titled, "Love Matters." Much was made of the phrase "theology matters" during and after the meeting of the 1994 General Assembly in Wichita. An obvious truth for Presbyterians, the phrase came to light in the assembly's report on the November 1993 "Re-Imagining" conference held in Minneapolis, but quickly became a weapon to be used against feminist theologies. As it came into vogue, I saw the phrase "theology matters" used as a put-down against any theological idea one did not like. Frequently we saw warnings against the ordination of gays and lesbians because "theology matters." "Love Matters" is theology, but theology that seeks to move beyond religious and ecclesiastical law and make love the measure of sexual ethics. I dedicate it "to Barbara and others who matter."

Love Matters:
1 Corinthians 13

If I speak in the tongues of heterosexuals or of angels, but have not love, I am a noisy gong or a clanging cymbal. And if I preach at Louisville headquarters,[1] and understand all definitive guidance and all authoritative interpretations of the Constitution, and if I have all Reformed faith, so as to remove mountains, but have not love, I am nothing. If I deny all I am, and if I deliver my patriarchal body to be burned, and have not love, I gain nothing.

Love is open and inclusive; love is not closeted or selective; it is not hostile or unjust. Love does not insist on its own orientation; it is not fearful or phobic; it does not rejoice in moralisms, but rejoices in freedom. Love bears all things, believes all things, hopes all things, endures all Presbyterians.

Love never ends; as for General Assemblies, they will pass away; as for permanent judicial commissions, they will cease; as for the *Book of Order*, it will pass away. For our confessions are imperfect and our ordinations are imperfect; but when the perfect comes, hierarchies will pass away. When I was a child, I spoke like a child, I thought like a child, I reasoned like a child; when I became an adult, I affirmed my sexuality. For now we see in a governing body dimly, but then whole sexual body to whole sexual body. Now I know in parts; then I shall understand in connections, even as I have been fully connected. So Bible, tradition, theology matter, these three; but what matters most is love.

Our Call for
Change and Thanksgiving

We love the Presbyterian Church (U.S.A.), and we love the many diverse faces of this community of faith. But we are increasingly sad and angry that this church, or any social institution, fails to see the face of its gay, lesbian, bisexual, and transgendered members and fails to see the face of injustice in its own attitudes and policies toward them. The church is still in the process of recovering from its blindness in upholding as Christian the institution of slavery and perpetuating the subordination of women as God's natural order of creation. How long until the church sees that our sexual orientation is morally neutral, that people are created by God for mutual love and sexual intimacy, and that committed, egalitarian relationships—whether the partners are gay, lesbian, bisexual, transgendered, or heterosexual—are blessings of God and gifts to the human community?

Chris Glaser, a gay Presbyterian who has been a clarion voice for justice in the church, wrote in a *Newsweek* editorial following the church's rejection of gay and lesbian ordination and a congressional vote against same-sex marriages: "I feel beaten up. . . . Had I been the victim of a street gay-bashing, I would be able to seek comfort from my church and legal redress from the government. When the gay-bashers are my own church and government, I'm bewildered, wondering where to turn."[2]

We who are heterosexuals bear responsibility for such abuses. "Heterosexism" is the term applied to the range of privileges that we enjoy—privileges of sanctioned intimate relationships, confirmation by our denomination as respectable enough for leadership, and the ordinary respect that people give each other in love and acceptance of our common humanity. We need to face the issue and face the problem; as Pogo said, "We have met the enemy, and it is us."

Gay, lesbian, bisexual, and transgendered people are not the problem. In demanding that others become heterosexual in order to be acceptable, it is *heterosexuals* who perpetuate an abusive, legalistic standard that is a violation of the biblical values of mercy, love, justice, and humility. Our ignorance of a whole history of Christian attitudes toward sexuality, and the development of antisex, antifemale standards of sexual relationship, continue to bind the church and each one of us, preventing our freedom and liberation to be the joyful, welcoming, justice-seeking people that God calls us to be.

Paul knew well the tensions between bondage and freedom, and the conflict produced by church efforts to ascertain which was which. Responding to whether male Gentiles first had to become circumcised before they could become Christian, Paul shakes up the church in Galatia and says: "Listen! I, Paul, am telling you that if you let yourselves be circumcised, Christ will be of no benefit to you. . . . You who want to be justified by the law have cut yourselves off from Christ; you have fallen away from grace. . . . For in Christ Jesus neither circumcision nor uncircumcision counts for anything; the only thing that counts is faith working through love" (Galatians 5:2–6). In this radical response, Paul calls the church to freedom, not for self-indulgence, but for following the one commandment that is the sum of the *whole* law: the commandment to love one another.

It seems to us that a simple test of whether we are being loving or not is that those whom we claim to love should *feel* loved. Gay, lesbian, bisexual, and transgendered people are not feeling the love of many Christians and churches. They are feeling isolated, excluded, devalued, and held to a standard of sexual morality that requires them to go against what they know as the integrity of their bodies. In the spirit and style of Paul, we, Mike and Sylvia, say to heterosexuals in the church: Listen! See the faces. Hear the words. Listen to the stories. Face your fears. Pray for the courage to change *yourselves*—your hearts and your minds and your restrictive church policies.

James B. Nelson, professor of Christian ethics at United Seminary of the Twin Cities, has published a sermon of gratitude to gay, lesbian, bisexual, and transgendered people titled "I Thank God for You."[3] We, too, thank God for these faces that have graced our lives, for their faith that has sustained our own, for their humor that has uplifted our spirits, for their caring that has warmed and embraced us, and for their passion that embodies Christ's love and justice in many-connected relations with others. We have been so blessed by their lives. We are so grateful to be a part of their journey. We have learned the joy of love and life in the company of this faithful, spirited people. May we live to see the day when gay, lesbian, bisexual, transgendered, and heterosexual people come face to face as brothers and sisters in Christ, partners in loving service to all God's people.

✦ Sylvia Thorson-Smith and Michael D. Smith live in Grinnell, Iowa, where Mike is pastor of the First Presbyterian Church and Sylvia is a lecturer in religious studies and sociology at Grinnell College. Sylvia is an ordained elder and member of the Grinnell church. They have three adult children, one grandson, and one Airedale terrier, who came into their home during the controversy over the 1991 sexuality report and, in the spirit of reform and feminism, is named Calvin Ruether.

Notes

Chapter 3:
Another Way: Speaking the Truth of Our Lives

1. Carolyn G. Heilbrun, *Writing a Woman's Life* (New York: Ballantine Books, 1988), 48.

2. Ibid., 118, emphasis added.

Chapter 17:
Facing Fears: "Cast Outs" Calling Us toward Healing

1. The story of Marta is representative of the lives of several lesbian women known by the author of this chapter.

2. Sharon Ringe, "A Gentile Woman's Story," in *Feminist Interpretation of the Bible,* ed. Letty Russell (Philadelphia: Westminster Press, 1985), 65–72.

Chapter 25:
"Facing" the Issue

1. A reference to the Reverend Jane Adams Spahr, a lesbian, being refused permission to preach at the daily chapel service at the Presbyterian national headquarters in Louisville, Kentucky.

2. Chris Glaser, *Newsweek,* September 16, 1996, p. 19.

3. This sermon by James Nelson is published in his book *Body Theology* (Louisville, Ky.: Westminster/John Knox Press, 1992).